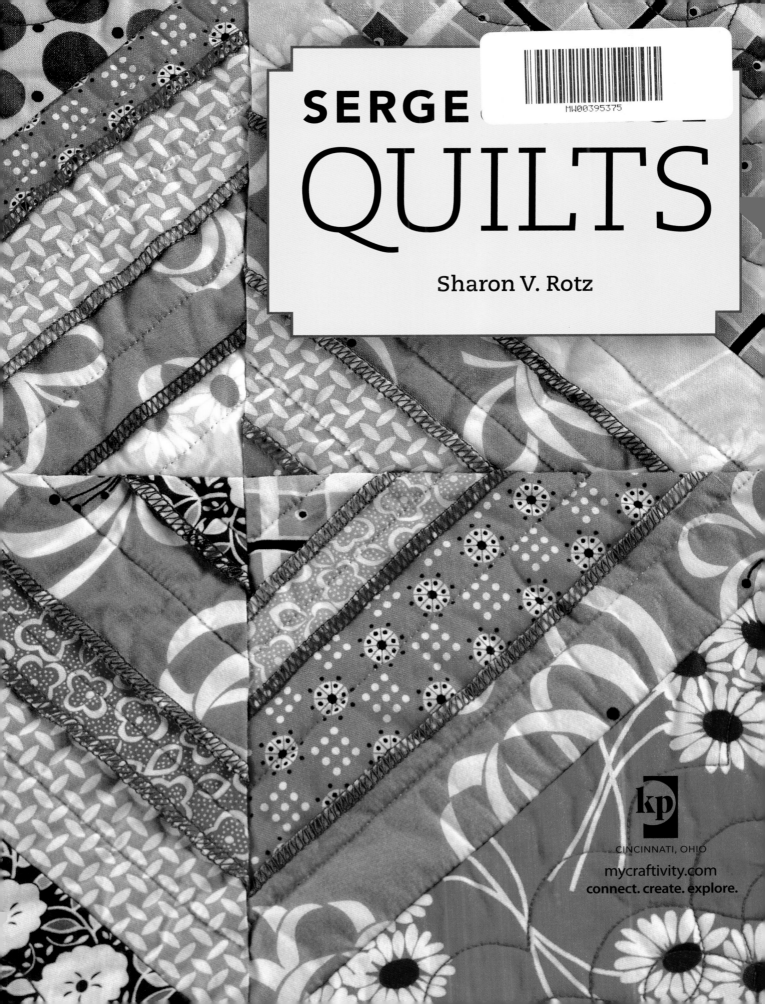

SERGE QUILTS

QUILTS

Sharon V. Rotz

kp

CINCINNATI, OHIO

mycraftivity.com
connect. create. explore.

Other fine Krause Publications titles are available from your local bookstore, craft supply store, online retailer or visit our website at www.fwmedia.com.

13 12 11 10 09   5 4 3 2 1

DISTRIBUTED IN CANADA BY
FRASER DIRECT
100 Armstrong Avenue
Georgetown, ON, Canada L7G 5S4
Tel: (905) 877-4411

DISTRIBUTED IN THE U.K. AND EUROPE
BY DAVID & CHARLES
Brunel House, Newton Abbot, Devon,
TQ12 4PU, England
Tel: (+44) 1626 323200,
Fax: (+44) 1626 323319
Email: postmaster@davidandcharles.co.uk

DISTRIBUTED IN AUSTRALIA BY
CAPRICORN LINK
P.O. Box 704, S. Windsor NSW, 2756
Australia
Tel: (02) 4577-3555

Library of Congress Cataloging in Publication Data
Rotz, Sharon V.
  Serge and merge quilts / Sharon V. Rotz.—1st ed.
      p. cm.
  Includes index.
  ISBN-13: 978-0-89689-810-3 (pbk. : alk. paper)
  ISBN-10: 0-89689-810-5 (pbk. : alk. paper)
  1. Quilting. 2. Serging. I. Title.
  TT835.R6758 2009
  746.46--dc22
                        2009001452

Edited by Liz Casler
Designed by Michelle Thompson
Production coordinated by Matt Wagner
Photography by Richard Deliantoni and
    Al Parrish

ABOUT THE AUTHOR

Between visits from her children and energetic grandchildren, Sharon enjoys sharing time with her husband Tom and being outdoors with their always enthusiastic dog Shadow. She is inspired by the beauty of central Wisconsin where she lives and divides her quilting time between traditional and art quilts.

Sharon has written two other Krause quilting books, *Log Cabin Quilts with Attitude* and *Quilting Through the Seasons*, and designs her own line of patterns by Sher. She has been commissioned by hospitals, museums and numerous private collectors and her quilts have received awards at national and international quilt shows.

Visit her at www.bysher.net.

ACKNOWLEDGMENTS

I would like to thank all the people who continuously help and support me, including:

My husband Tom and the rest of my family who constantly encourage me

Candy Wiza, who worked with me on the idea for the book, Liz Casler, Michelle Thompson, Vanessa Lyman and the rest of the Krause Publications staff who helped with the production of this book

Nancy Zieman and Deanna Springer whose valuable expertise guided me as we worked on the DVD

The many quilters, both old friends and new, who stimulate me and stretch me out in new directions

Metric Conversion Chart

TO CONVERT	TO	MULTIPLY BY
Inches	Centimeters	2.54
Centimeters	Inches	0.4
Feet	Centimeters	30.5
Centimeters	Feet	0.03
Yards	Meters	0.9
Meters	Yards	1.1

CONTENTS

INTRODUCTION

Yes, I have a serger. I used it to clean finish the hem of my pants, and it made wonderful seams on my last drapery project. I think my serger is under that stack of fabric in the corner of my studio. I was going to use it for repairing my T-shirt, but it seemed too much trouble to get it out and in working order, so I just zigzagged the T-shirt seam on my sewing machine. You see, I am a quilter now, and I don't have time for all those other sewing projects.

So my serger sat, forlorn and forgotten, covered with a pile of quilting fabric and a layer of dust. One day I was madly digging through my stash, searching for that perfect fabric to work into my current project. I spotted more quilting fabric in the corner, and as I searched through my possible choices, I unearthed my serger.

Later, as I cut and stitched my quilt blocks, I kept thinking about my serger. I should be using it. Would there be a way I could use my serger to make quilts? That day I challenged myself to think of my serger as a quilting tool.

Of course, it wouldn't be a replacement for my trusted sewing machine; the machine does whatever I command it to do from the beginning to the end of my quilting project. But, just as I have specialty rulers to complement my all-purpose 6" x 24" ruler, I could use my serger as a specialty machine to complement my sewing machine. There are embroidery machines and long-arm quilting machines to broaden our quilting endeavors. Let's add the serger to that list.

Soon, I was serging away and merging that serging into my quilting projects. Because the serger seams, neatly trims threads and overcast seams, I could use it to piece my quilts. And, it should be mentioned, that it does this with a nice ¼" seam allowance. I could go beyond the basic overlock stitch, and use other serging stitches to add variety and decorative detail to my serged and merged quilts. The serger handles the specialty threads and fabrics that can be difficult on my conventional sewing machine so I could breeze on to more unique and original quilts.

My hope is that *Serge & Merge Quilts* will challenge you to find that dark corner of your closet where your serger is hiding. Dust it off, oil it up and start your journey with your new quilting tool. For those of you who are already able-bodied serging fanatics, enjoy the fun of adding quilt-making to your list of serger skills.

NOTES FROM NANCY

As part of the Create with Nancy line, this book contains extra, helpful tips and a bonus DVD from sewing and craft expert Nancy Zieman. When you encounter a Note from Nancy, stop to read it! And be sure to watch the DVD to see the techniques in action!

CHAPTER 1

TECHNIQUES & MATERIALS

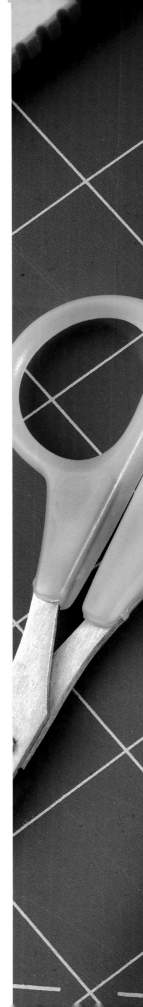

I know two kinds of quilters, those who test the waters and research the subject thoroughly before they start, and those who jump in first and only go back to the basics when they are deep into a project.

For those of you who are like my good friend "the researcher," the following section will start you on your exploration of serging and merging quilts. For others, who are like me, "the jumper," this section will be a reference guide to help you out of the deep and murky waters of the unknown.

However, no matter how you get here, this section is a treasure chest of tips and know-how. Here you will look at the serger itself and the common serging tools. You will find the basic serging stitches described in detail. Finally, you will review quilting basics: tips for fabric selection, quilting terms and tools, and finishing techniques.

SETTING UP THE SERGER

PARTS OF THE SERGER

The serger is a high-speed machine that is able to seam, trim and finish the raw edges of your fabrics all in one operation. It differs from a sewing machine, which has a needle and a bobbin, because a serger has needle threads (often more than one) and loopers. Sergers can operate with as few as two threads and as many as four or more threads.

The projects in this book are made with the typical stitches of a four-thread serger. A great amount of the serging is done at the normal "N," or typical, setting of the serger, making it more comfortable for many quilters who are timid about making adjustments to their machines. However, for some operations and for variety in some projects, I've indicated changes.

Check your owner's manual to locate the following parts of your serger. You will need to recognize the **left needle position**, the **right needle position**, the **upper looper** and the **lower looper** and how to adjust the **thread tensions** for each of these.

You can make changes to the **stitch length** to create dense or more open stitches. Locate the dial, usually on the side of the machine, for changing the stitch length. Like your conventional sewing machine stitching, most of your serging is done at the normal "N" stitch length.

The **serger blades** trim the edge of the fabric as you serge. In some cases, you will be stitching close to a fabric fold, and you will not want to cut the fabric. Check your owner's manual to see if your moving blade can be disengaged and for instructions on how to do this.

The **stitch finger** is a small metal finger on the throat plate over which the stitches form when serging. On my serger, for overlock stitching the stitch finger is in the "N" position. When stitching a rolled edge, I set the stitch finger at the "R" setting, moving the stitch finger so the threads loop tightly around the fabric edge. You will want to check your manual for the correct settings for overlock and rolled edge stitches.

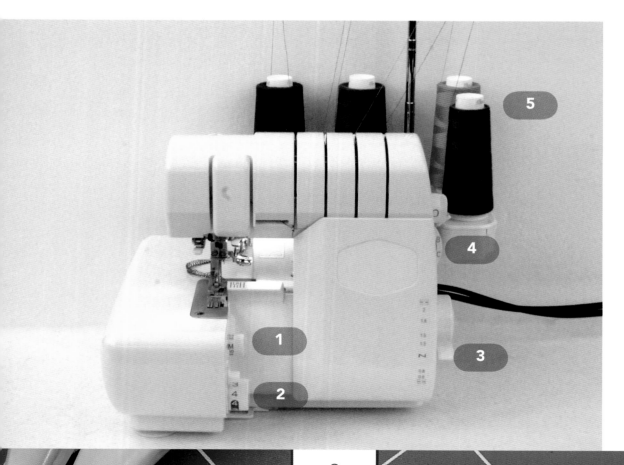

PARTS OF A SERGER
1. Stitch width dial
2. Stitch length dial
3. Differential feed adjustment lever
4. Overlock stitch selector
5. Thread spools

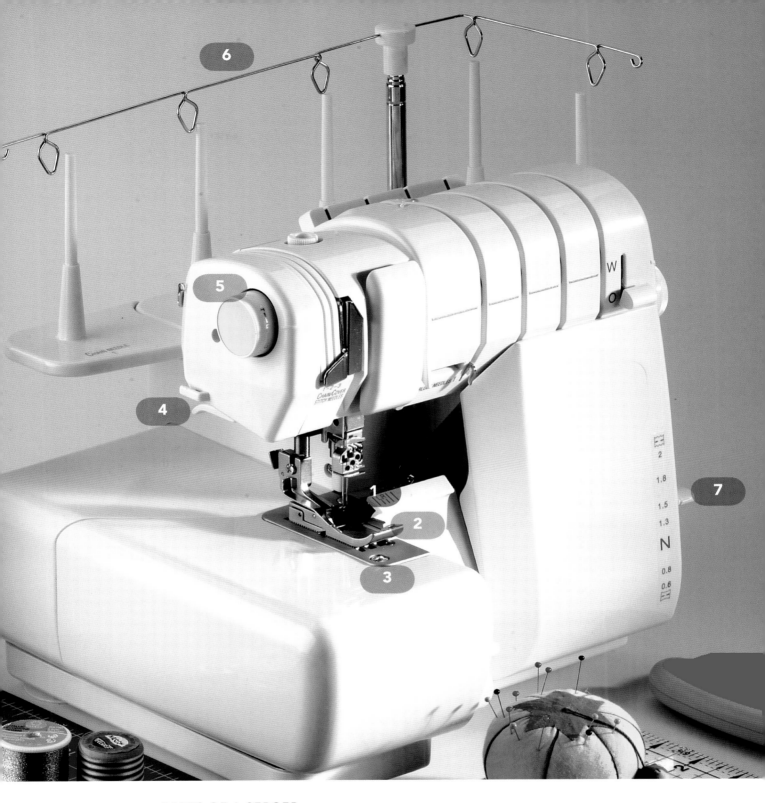

PARTS OF A SERGER
1. Needles
2. Presser foot
3. Throat plate
4. Thread cutter
5. Chain/Cover stitch tension dial
6. Telescopic threading guide
7. Differential feed adjustment lever

SERGER TOOLS

For maintaining your serger, you will need a **cleaning brush** to control the thread and lint buildup. Always clean your serger before oiling. **Oil** will keep your serger running smoothly. Use lightweight oil made for sergers as general household oil is too heavy.

Small screwdrivers will help to loosen the plates and blades for cleaning and replacement. The **Allen wrench** loosens the needle screw for changing your needles. Always tighten both needle screws even if you are stitching with only one needle. The machine's vibrations may cause a loose screw to fall out and become lost. Keep a supply of **serger needles**. You will want to use the proper type and size needle with different threads for top performance.

Sergers require at least two threads, and in most cases more than two threads, for operating. You will want a good supply of **threads** including a variety of specialty threads. **Cone and spool holders** will help keep your threads feeding correctly. **Thread nets** will keep slippery threads from sliding down and getting caught under the spool. **Tweezers** are very helpful to catch threads and feed them through areas where your fingers won't fit. **Seam sealant** applied to the ends of the threads will prevent unraveling seams and edges.

For two-thread serging, you will need a **two-thread converter**. This small attachment fits over the upper looper with a small pin that fits into the looper eye. This is a standard feature on some sergers and an optional accessory for others. Check your manual to determine if your serger can create a two-thread overlock. You may also want **specialized feet** for different serging operations. A **dust cover**, either cloth or vinyl, will protect your serger when not in use.

MAINTAINING THE SERGER

The kindest things you can do for your serger are to keep it cleaned and oiled. Start by cleaning off that layer of dust that has accumulated on your machine since the last time you used it. Turn off the power or unplug the machine so there isn't a chance that it will "come alive" during your maintenance operations. Clean out the bits of threads and lint that remind you of the last project you were serging. Opening up the serger covers and removing the throat plate will expose areas, making them easier to clean. A stiff brush will clean many areas. A vacuum cleaner works well for removing threads, but take care, as it may also remove any accessories that lie close by. A small handheld vacuum with an easy-to-remove dust tray is a better choice so you do not have to dig into a large dust bag for that "swallowed" serger part.

If your serger has been waiting a long time for its chance to shine, it may start off with a few squeaks and creaks. Grab the oil bottle and consult your owner's manual to lubricate those sliding parts and joints to keep them moving smoothly and easily. With a machine that performs at a level of 1,300 to 1,500 stitches per minute (about twice the speed of a conventional sewing machine), you will be able to zip through projects with ease using a well-oiled machine.

Just as your sewing machine works better with a new needle, your serger will also work better with the sharp point and the straight shaft of a new needle. Keep your needle threaded as you remove it from your machine. This will prevent it from disappearing into the serger if you lose your grip. Some machines have a tool to help with inserting a needle. Many sergers use the same needles as your sewing machine, but some do not. Check the type of needle needed for your serger and the correct way to insert it.

Clean the serger cutting blades and lightly lubricate with a drop of oil. Check if the blades are nicked or dull. Follow the manual directions or take your serger to a dealer for blade replacement. Even with good home maintenance, periodic checkups by your dealer are important for top performance and a long serger life.

SERGER TOOLS
1. Thread
2. Spool holders
3. Cone holders
4. Cleaning brush
5. Small screwdrivers
6. Thread net
7. Seam ripper/scissors

To secure serger thread tails, I sparingly use a liquid seam sealant. To speed up the drying process, press the tail end with the tip of an iron before clipping off the excess thread. This is a great time saver.

NOTES FROM **NANCY**

CHOOSING THREADS

Because the serger will stitch with a great variety of threads, you can use the specialty threads that often cause grief on the standard sewing machine. The spools or cones can be placed right on the machine for use in the upper or lower loopers. You will not be limited to the small amount of decorative thread that can be wound on the bobbin of your sewing machine.

All-purpose polyester serging thread is a popular choice for general serging needs. It is a lightweight two-ply thread that is less bulky for the multiple thread serged seams. It comes on cones that are cross-wound for the high speeds of serging.

The **50 wt cotton spools or cones** that we use on our sewing machine can also work well on our sergers. Use a spool cap to prevent the thread from becoming caught on or around the bottom of the spool. In addition to 50 wt, **40 wt cotton and cotton machine quilting threads** can be used. These heavier three-ply threads add body to the seams and are showier when the seams are exposed on the right side of the fabric.

Just as they do for your machine embroidery and quilting, **rayon threads and polyester specialty threads** such as trilobal polyesters give a luster and sheen to your projects especially when used in the loopers. Use a thread net to keep the threads from sliding down and getting caught under the cone.

Even though they are used mainly on stretchy fabrics, **wooly nylon and Polyarn** can be used on your quilts. They have a very soft feel, and they puff up and look thick on your serged project.

The **metallic threads** that often cause problems on your conventional sewing machine can be used much more easily in the loopers of your serger. They will give a sparkly, decorative touch to your wall quilt.

Even thicker threads like **perle cotton** work well in the loopers. They give a bold look to a rolled hem and are available in a wide variety of colors. Since they are usually not wound on cones, you may have to rewind onto a cone so they feed easily. The distinctive look of the heavy threads is definitely worth the effort.

Always test your stitches. Keep plenty of muslin at your machine for testing the stitches so you won't be tempted to skip this important step. After testing on muslin, test on a scrap of fabric from your project in case any minor adjustments are needed. Check your needle and the tension for your thread combination. Even though a variety of threads work great, a different needle type or size may be required, or the tensions may need adjusting to make perfect stitches.

Also, do a pressing test on your threads for melting points. Specialty threads may lose their luster or melt completely if pressed with a hot iron. It is a good choice to use a pressing cloth if you need to press over specialty threads.

THREADING THE SERGER

Is this the reason you are not using the full potential of your serger? Do you feel that if your serger becomes unthreaded, you are lost? Today's sergers are much easier to thread than earlier models. Some even zip the thread through the loopers without any effort on the operator's part.

When threading the serger from the start, order is everything. The order in which the serger is threaded is quite important to keep the threads from twisting and breaking when you make that first stitch. (Where was this information when I was threading my first serger with the "happy accident" approach? I was happy when I accidentally threaded my serger correctly.) This is the threading order for most sergers, but you should check your manual for the correct order for your serger.

Tying On

When you're ready to replace a cone that's already threaded in the serger, the tying-on method for threading usually works well for all-purpose threads. Clip the thread close to the cone you are removing. Tie the thread onto the new thread and gently pull through the serger. Raise the presser foot and loosen the tensions when doing this. Since you probably feel more comfortable threading the needles, you can use this method just for the loopers. Tying on can be used for the needle threads, but the knot will not pull through the needle. Cut the knot at the needle and thread the needle.

Step 1: When threading the serger from scratch, start by threading the upper looper. Often there is a small diagram inside of the cover of the serger to help, or consult that ever-popular owner's manual.

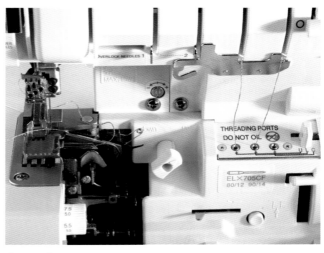

Step 2: Second, thread the lower looper. It's important that the lower looper thread is crossing over the upper looper. Go back and check that the threads have not come out of any of the guides.

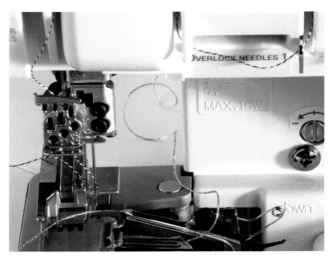

Step 3: Now it's time to thread the needles, starting with the right needle. You do not want the needle threads to run under the looper threads, which will also cause the threads to break. Check to make sure the thread antenna is in the highest position and your threads are engaged between the tension discs.

PRACTICING STITCHES

The goal of this book is not to teach you how to use your serger but to offer you options for using your serger as a quilting tool. In this section, we will look at the serging stitches used on the projects in this book. Use your owner's manual as the ultimate source of specific information on your serger. Other resources containing serging tips and techniques may also be helpful.

In this book, there are serger setup suggestions listed for each project. These were based on my serger, fabrics and thread choices. As often as possible, my serger was used at the normal "N" settings (your serger may not have an "N" setting—refer to your manual for average settings). These settings may need to be adjusted for your serger. Always test your stitches on extra pieces of fabric from your project to fine-tune the settings for your serger.

OVERLOCK STITCH

FOUR-THREAD OVERLOCK STITCH
This is the most commonly used serging stitch. The four-thread overlock stitch seams with the benefit of a security stitch. It trims the edge of the fabric and overcasts it to finish the fabric edge. The beauty of this is that it does it all in one sewing operation. This is the stitch that has made serging a popular choice for a variety of fabrics, both woven and knit. For the four-thread overlock stitch, your serger settings will usually all be set at "N" (normal or average). For a perfect stitch, the looper threads will interlock right at the edge of the fabric, pulling neither to the front nor the back of the fabric. The needle threads will be visible on the right side of the fabric and almost invisible on the wrong side of the fabric.

Because of the rapid speed of the serger and the strength of the seams, serging can often replace your sewing machine for putting your quilt together. The four-thread overlock stitch is normally ¼" wide, making it perfect for stitching quilter's ¼" seams. Test your serger before seaming. To use this option, run the fabric right at the edge of the cutting blade only trimming off raveled threads. Your seams will be less likely to ravel or pull apart because the seam edge is finished. You will also have fewer stray threads shadowing through on the front of your light-colored quilts.

Gathering or "ruching" can be done very quickly on your serger. There will be no need for the several stitching steps often done to gather on your conventional sewing machine. You can do it all in one step on your serger. If your serger has settings for gathering, follow your manual's instructions. Otherwise, use the familiar four-thread overlock stitch. Lengthen the stitches, tighten the tension of both needles, and, like magic, ruffles feed out of your serger. If you would like to increase the fullness of the ruffle, simply hold your fingers on the fabric behind the presser foot. This prevents the fabric from feeding through as easily thus increasing the amount of fabric in the ruffle. If the ruffles are still not full enough, pull the right needle thread to further gather. (Be careful that you don't pull the thread completely out or your ruffles will be quickly undone!)

WIDE THREE-THREAD OVERLOCK STITCH

To change from a four-thread overlock stitch to a wide three-thread overlock stitch, remove the right needle. Leave the needle threaded when removing to prevent the needle from accidentally falling into the machine, making it difficult to retrieve. Some sergers may have a tool to hold the needle when you are removing or replacing it.

As with the four-thread overlock stitch, the upper and lower looper threads should interlock right on the edge of the fabric and the needle thread is visible on the right side of the fabric. The advantage of the three-thread overlock stitch is that it uses less thread, which makes the seams less bulky. The seams will be secure for quilting projects since your quilting stitches will also be there to add strength and sturdiness to the quilt.

The wide three-thread overlock stitch can be used for quilter's ¼" seams. (Test your serger seam for accuracy.) The seams can be stitched with the right sides of the fabrics together resulting in typical seam allowances on the wrong side of the fabric. The seams can also be stitched with the wrong sides of the fabrics together resulting in decorative seams on the right side of the fabric. Many of the quilts in this book use the second option. The seams can be left dimensional (sticking up on the surface) as they are in *Thirteen's a Charm*, or they can be quilted (stitched down in the quilting process) for a flatter appearance as in *Mixed Bouquet*.

NARROW THREE-THREAD OVERLOCK STITCH

To change from a wide to a narrow three-thread overlock stitch, remove the needle from the left needle position and place it in the right needle position. Remember when removing, a threaded needle is less likely to become a disappearing needle!

The narrow three-thread overlock stitch will normally stitch sturdy seams on medium to tightly woven fabrics. More often, the narrow overlock stitch is used for decorative seaming or edge finishing with specialty threads.

TWO-THREAD OVERLOCK STITCH

A two-thread overlock can be used for a soft decorative finish. To stitch a two-thread overlock stitch, the upper looper is covered with a two-thread converter. Check your owner's manual to see if your serger can be used with only two threads, and for the correct setup for your machine. If a two-thread stitch is not possible, use with a narrow three-thread overlock stitch.

If you see an "M" on your stitch length dial, it refers to the term marrowing—an industrial sewing term meaning ¼" seam.

NOTES FROM **NANCY**

FLATLOCK STITCH

The flatlock stitch can be used for seaming two fabrics together, but it is often used as a decorative accent to your fabric. By folding your fabric and stitching along that folded edge, this serging stitch can be used in the center of your fabric rather than only on the edge. When stitching the flatlock stitch, guide your fabric so that approximately half of the stitch is extending beyond the folded edge of the fabric. Your serger may have a special foot that holds the folded fabric in position so that the stitching extends over the edge. You do not want to cut your fabric, so stitch carefully and disengage the cutting blade, if possible.

After the serging is done, pull the fabric open until the stitches lie flat. When the fabrics are flatlock stitched with the wrong sides of the fabrics together, the looper thread is visible on the right side of the fabric. This may be referred to as the looper stitch. When the fabrics are flatlock stitched with the right sides of the fabrics together, the needle thread is visible on the right side of the fabric. This is referred to as the ladder stitch.

The flatlock stitch may be used to join two fabrics together. The stitching may be extended beyond the fabric edge as with the decorative flatlock stitching. Using medium weight quilter's cottons, I have had good results guiding the fabric right along the cutting blade. This second option forms a stronger seam that will be less likely to pull apart. Again, test the options on your serger.

Tip

Always test your serging on scraps of your project fabrics. Remember to lower your presser foot and have the tensions at the proper settings for your stitch. Make any needed adjustments to the tensions based on your combination of the thread and fabric. The suggested tensions for the projects in this book are based on the threads and fabrics I chose. They may need to be changed slightly for your serger.

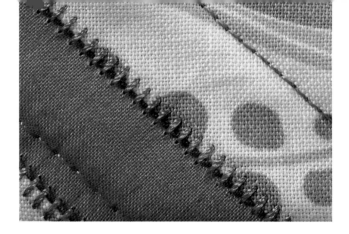

THREE-THREAD FLATLOCK STITCH

The flatlock stitch may be stitched with the left needle only, making a wider stitch, or may be stitched with the right needle only making a narrow flatlock stitch. Generally, the needle tension is loosened, and the lower looper tension is tightened (check your manual for specifics). Testing is required to see what tension settings will allow the stitch to lie the flattest. Your thread and fabric choices will make the difference. The stitch length can be adjusted to make the stitches longer, giving the stitch a more open look, or shorter, creating a denser line.

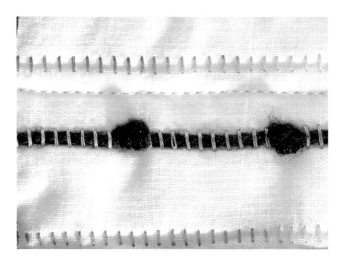

TWO-THREAD FLATLOCK STITCH

A two-thread flatlock stitch is more economical, using one less spool of thread and creating a softer stitch. To stitch a two-thread flatlock stitch, you will need to cover the upper looper with the two-thread converter. This converter may be built in or it may be an optional accessory that is attached to the upper looper with the tip inserted into the eye of the upper looper. Check your owner's manual to see if your serger can be used with only two threads and for the correct setup for your serger.

ROLLED EDGE

A rolled edge finish is a very narrow finish where, just as the name implies, the fabric edge is rolled under and closely overcast with the looper thread. You will set up your machine by removing the left needle and moving the stitch finger to the "R" setting (many machines have this setting marked on the foot). The "R" or rolled edge setting moves the stitch finger, allowing the fabric to roll as you stitch. Check your owner's manual for specific instructions for setting up your serger for a rolled edge.

This finish is best suited for lighter-weight or tightly woven fabrics. Even though rolling the fabric edge makes it a strong finish, you still may not be catching enough fabric to prevent the stitching from pulling off heavier or coarser fabrics. This stitch is especially showy with the use of the many decorative threads available.

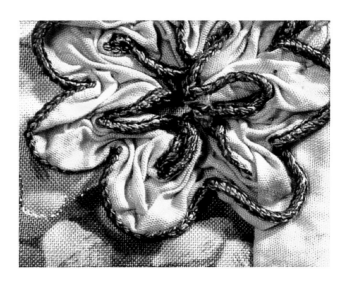

TWO-THREAD ROLLED EDGE

Again, by removing one thread, you will have less bulk and use less thread. For a two-thread rolled edge, you will need to attach the two-thread converter on the upper looper. You will be stitching with the right needle thread and the lower looper thread.

THREE-THREAD ROLLED EDGE

For a three-thread rolled edge, you will be stitching only with the right needle in the serger, and you will have the stitch finger in the "R" setting. The lower looper thread is tightened so the upper looper thread wraps around the rolled edge of the fabric. The upper looper thread is the thread seen on the fabric edge. Specialty threads may be used in the upper looper to add a creative touch to your serged edge.

With most threads, the stitch length is decreased so the stitches form a dense edge treatment. For heavier threads such as perle cotton, the stitch length may not need to be adjusted or it may need to be lengthened slightly to prevent a buildup of thread.

QUILTING TOOLS & EQUIPMENT

Our conventional **sewing machine** is our most versatile quilting tool. Keep it cleaned and oiled for top performance. Don't forget to take it to your dealer for routine maintenance to avoid problems when you are experiencing an especially creative moment. Select **specialty feet**, such as a ¼" foot and its many friends, that make sewing a treat rather than a chore.

Threads and needles go together. Select a needle that fits your thread choice, and you will avoid frustrating skipped stitches and broken threads. Dull and bent needles will only result in poor quality stitching and may damage your machine. Keep a supply of new needles and don't hesitate to make the change.

Rotary cutters, rulers and **mats** make fabric cutting quick and easy. Choose a larger mat to avoid excessive folding when cutting a strip. Keep a sharp blade in your cutter and keep the cutter closed so that sharp blade will only be used on your fabric and not your fingers or

dropped on bare toes. The most useful ruler is a 6" × 24" ruler, and if I had only one ruler, this would be my choice. Square rulers are very helpful to size blocks. There are numerous other rulers available that make many complicated cuts much easier.

Any sewing studio would be lost without a variety of basic sewing tools, including **large sewing scissors** and **small thread clippers, straight pins, safety pins** for quilt basting and a **seam ripper**. Plan an area to store these and the rest of your sewing tools so they will be at your fingertips, ready to be used.

An **iron** and a **firm pressing surface** are another quilter's necessity. Keep these close to your sewing machine so it is convenient to press as you stitch. A **press cloth** is helpful to protect your project and the bottom of your iron. Test your fabrics, threads and fusible webs for the best results.

QUILTING TOOLS & EQUIPMENT
1. Iron
2. Sewing machine
3. Scissors
4. Thread clippers
5. Specialty feet
6. Safety pins
7. Thread
8. Seam ripper
9. Mat
10. Small rotary cutter
11. Straight pins
12. Square ruler
13. Rotary cutter

SELECTING FABRIC

Choosing fabrics is one of the most enjoyable parts of making a quilt. Here you can express your individuality by selecting colors and designs that reflect your particular style. Do you love bright and scrappy, sleek and sophisticated, or soft and serene? The fabrics you see in the projects of this book are only suggestions and a mere stepping-off point for making your own personal selections.

For that scrappy look, more is better. Choose fabrics including a multitude of colors, combining large and small prints, checks, plaids, geometrics, dots and stripes. For a sleek and sophisticated look, try the simplicity and drama of a high-contrast, two-color quilt. For a calm and tranquil look, choose muted or low-contrast fabrics of an analogous (or neighboring) color scheme.

Cotton fabrics are a favorite of quilters. Fabrics of 100 percent cotton press well and ease into the seams nicely. Because you are investing a good amount of time and effort into making your quilted project, choose high-quality cottons, such as those found in quilt shops. Organic cottons and bamboo fabrics as seen in *Simply Leafy* offer an earth-friendly choice for quilts. Specialty fabrics, including silks and rayons, offer creative options for your quilts.

Along with your fabric choices, you also have a wide range of batting options. Cotton has been a perennial favorite for its usability and comfort. The rough surface texture of cotton and cotton blends helps them cling to the quilt top, making them easy to machine-quilt. You can choose from unbleached batts, which work well under most fabrics colors, to bleached batting for use with white quilt tops and black to use under dark fabrics. Wool batting and newer eco-friendly bamboo batting also quilt very well and are good choices.

BASTING: large stitches made by hand or machine designed to hold the fabrics together until the permanent stitching is done.

SEAM ALLOWANCE: the width of the fabric from the seam line stitching to the raw edge of the fabric. In this book, the seam allowances are ¼" unless otherwise noted.

STRATA: a striped set of fabrics pieced from fabric strips of different colors and patterns. Triangles or other shapes can then be cut from the strata rather than cutting and piecing numerous small pieces. The strips can be equal width strips or varying widths such as in *Thirteen's a Charm*.

TRIANGLES: three-sided shapes used as a basis for many pieced blocks.

Half-square triangles are made by cutting a square diagonally from corner to corner resulting in two equal right angle triangles. Half-square triangles are combined with strata triangles in *Thirteen's a Charm*.

Quarter-square triangles are made by crosscutting a square diagonally into four equal triangles each having one right angle. Most often quarter-square triangles of two (or more) colors are re-pieced to make the block, but in the background of *Spinning Pinwheels* quarter-square triangles of the same fabric are re-pieced after adding the pinwheels.

Equilateral triangles are triangles with three equal sides and equal angles. They can be cut from a fabric strip by alternating the base on the bottom and the top of the strip. Equilateral triangles are often combined with diamonds and hexagons such as in *Alice's Flower Garden*.

SQUARING HALF-SQUARE TRIANGLE BLOCKS

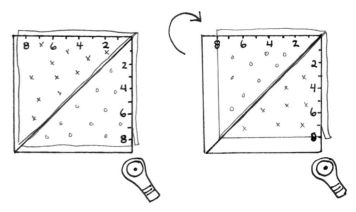

For a right-handed person: Turn your block so the diagonal seam runs from lower left to upper right. Place the diagonal line of your square on the seam line with the zero corner on the top right. Trim the right side and top of the block. Turn the block 180 degrees, place the cut edges on the desired size (8" illustrated) and trim the two remaining sides.

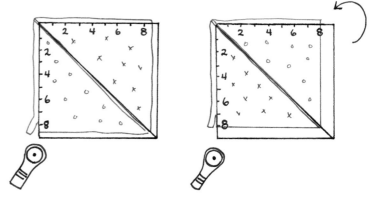

For a left-handed person: Turn your block so the diagonal seam runs from upper left to lower right. Place the diagonal line of your square on the seam line with the zero corner on the top left. Trim the left side and top of the block. Turn the block 180 degrees, place the cut edges on the desired size (8" illustrated) and trim the two remaining sides.

BINDINGS

LAYERING

Layering for quilting involves layering the backing wrong side up, the batting and the quilt top right side up. Place the backing on the surface as straight as possible. Tape or clip it taut without stretching. Smooth the batting over the backing. Position the quilt top over the batting, taking care to keep horizontal and vertical lines straight and corners square. Using small safety pins about 4"–6" apart, pin baste the quilt for machine quilting. Hand baste around the edges of the quilt, keeping the basting inside of the ¼" seam allowance where it will be covered by the binding.

CONTINUOUS BINDING

A narrow, ¼" wide binding that finishes the edge by enclosing it in a double fabric strip that goes completely around the quilt.

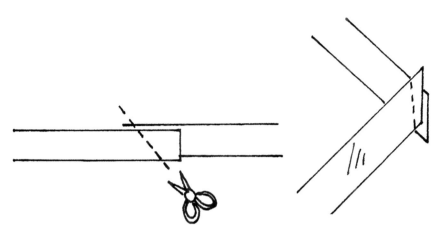

PREPARING THE BINDING:

1: Cut the binding strips 2" wide on the straight or bias grainline. Cut enough strips to exceed the perimeter of the quilt.

2: Overlap the ends of two strips, both right side up, and cut at an angle. By cutting through both strips the angle will be the same and need not be a 45-degree angle.

3: Align the strips at the ¼" seam allowance and stitch a diagonal seam. Using a diagonal seam will spread the bulk of the seam allowance in the binding strip.

4: Piece additional strips until the length of the binding is 6" longer than the quilt circumference. Press the seam allowances open.

ADDING THE BINDING:

1: Add the binding after you have finished quilting the project. Press the binding in half lengthwise with wrong sides together making a 1" wide strip.

2: On the right side of the quilt, match the raw edges of the binding to the raw edge of the quilt top. Start the binding midway on one side of the quilt, leaving a 3" unstitched tail of binding. Stitch a ¼" seam to attach the binding to the quilt.

MITERING THE CORNERS:

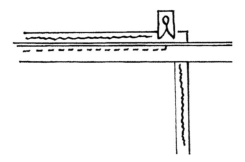 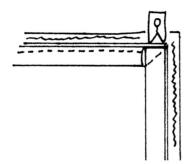 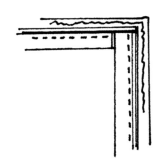

1: Stop stitching ¼" before the corner of the quilt. With the needle down, pivot the quilt to align with the second side of the quilt. Backstitch to the edge of the quilt top, roughly 4 or 5 stitches.

2: With the needle down, raise the presser foot and fold the binding back to the needle and even with the second edge of the quilt. A stiletto or seam ripper may be helpful for this task. A 45-degree miter will form under the fold.

3: Stitch along the second side of the quilt and continue adding the binding around the quilt.

JOINING THE ENDS OF THE BINDING:

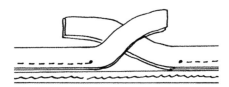  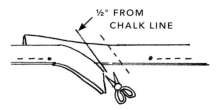

1: Stop stitching the binding 3"–4" from the starting point. Remove the quilt from the machine.

2: Trim the starting end on a diagonal. It is not necessary to open the folded binding. Lay this end over the finish end and draw a pencil or chalk line at the overlap.

3: Trim the binding ½" longer than the drawn line.

 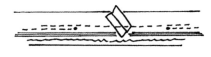 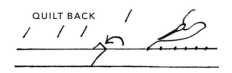

4: Align the folded binding ends at the ¼" seam line and stitch. Backstitch at the folded edge. Open the seam allowance.

5: The binding will now fit the quilt edge. Stitch the binding in place, overlapping the previous seams to secure the stitching.

6: Trim the excess batting and backing even with the quilt top. If a rod pocket is desired, add the rod pocket to the top of the quilt back.

7: Turn the binding to the back of the quilt encasing the raw edges and hand stitch. Fold the binding to form a folded miter at the back corners. Trim or tuck under the seam allowance tail.

BINDING WITH OVERLAPPED CORNERS

One side of the quilt is bound, turned to the back and hand stitched before the adjacent side is bound.

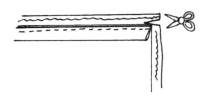 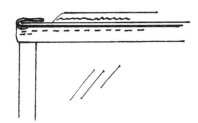 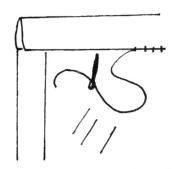

1: Cut the binding strips 2" wide. With wrong sides together, press the binding in half lengthwise making a 1" wide strip.

2: Match the raw edges of the underlap binding to the edge of the quilt. Start stitching the binding on at the corner edge of the quilt. Stitch a ¼" seam. Stitch to the opposite corner of the quilt and off the edge. Trim the batting and backing even with the quilt. If this is the top of the quilt and you would like a rod pocket, add it at this time.

3: Repeat on the opposite edge of the quilt. Turn the binding to the back and hand-stitch before attaching the overlap binding.

4: Match the raw edges of the overlap binding to the edge of the quilt. Extend the binding ½"–¾" beyond the edge of the quilt. Fold the end of the overlap binding snugly around the edge to the back of the quilt. This will encase the previously bound edge of the quilt. Use a ¼" seam to stitch the binding to the quilt edge. Before you stitch off the opposite end, trim the binding ½"–¾" longer than the quilt. Fold the binding around to the quilt back. Finish stitching the binding to the quilt edge, catching in the binding that was folded to the back.

5: Trim the batting and backing. If this is the top of the quilt, add a rod pocket, if desired. Turn the binding to the quilt back and hand-stitch the binding and folded ends.

6: Repeat on the opposite edge of the quilt.

FACED BINDING

No binding is visible on the right side of the quilt since the entire binding is pressed to the back of the quilt.

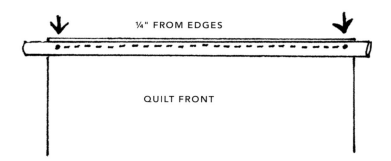

¼" FROM EDGES

QUILT FRONT

1: Cut the binding strips 2" wide. Piece, if needed, pressing the seam allowances open. With wrong sides together, press the binding lengthwise making a 1" strip.

2: Cut the binding 2" longer than the side of the quilt. Center the binding on the right side of the quilt with the raw edges even. Start stitching at a dot ¼" from the end of the quilt. Stitch the binding to the side of the quilt stopping ¼" from the end of the quilt. Backstitch at the start and finish of the stitching.* Trim excess batting and backing.

3: Continue in the same manner, adding binding to the remaining three sides of the quilt.

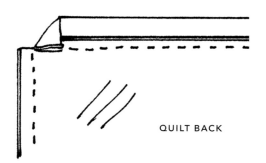

QUILT BACK

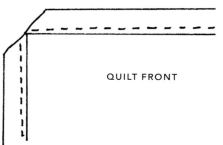

QUILT FRONT

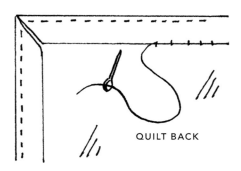

QUILT BACK

4: Press the binding toward the seam allowance. Press under 45-degree folds on the ends of the stitching.

5: Machine-stitch close to the seamed edge of the binding only stitching through the binding and the seam allowance (this understitching technique is often used in garment construction to help facings lie flat).

6: Press the entire binding to the back of the quilt. Hand-stitch the folded edge of the binding to the back of the quilt. Hand-stitch the mitered corners.

*Note: When combining binding techniques such as in *Thirteen's a Charm*, stitch the binding on the entire length of the quilt side instead of stopping ¼" from the ends.

ROD POCKETS

Add the rod pocket to the top of your quilt back after you have stitched the binding to the quilt and have trimmed off the excess batting and backing.*

FUSE ENDS

  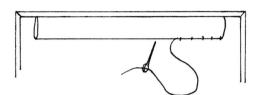

QUILT BACK

1: Cut a fabric strip 8½" wide by 2" less than the width of your quilt. Finish the short ends of the rod pocket by folding under ½" and fusing with a short piece of fusible web. With wrong sides together, press the fabric strip in half lengthwise.

2: Center the rod pocket on the quilt back with raw edges even with the top of the quilt. Stitch the rod pocket to the quilt. You will be stitching over the same seam that attached the binding to the quilt front.

3: Hand-stitch the bottom of the rod pocket to the back of the quilt. Be careful that your stitches do not show through on the front of your quilt.

*Note: In some quilts, such as *Simply Leafy* and *Berries and Blooms*, appliqué or other details are added after the binding is finished. Instead of adding the rod pocket in the binding, hand-stitch the rod pocket to the back of the quilt after all details are completed. Stitch the rod pocket into a tube. Hide the seam on the underside of the tube when hand-stitching the rod pocket to the back of the quilt.

LABELS

Why was this quilt made? Did it mark a special occasion in a person's life? Were the pieces cut from a valued collection or from a treasured piece of clothing? Was there a story or bit of poetry that influenced the design of this quilt? What is the fiber content of the fabrics, threads and batting? What is the best way to care for this quilt? And, the most important questions of all: Who made this quilt and when was it made?

The answers to any or all of the above questions can be added to a quilt's label. In the future, you and others who treasure your quilt will be happy to have this information. (We can't always remember all the details.) Quilts are not just bits of fabric and batting to keep us warm, they are priceless possessions that tell the tales of the lives of their makers and recipients.

Simple labels can be made from fabric scraps with fabric-safe markers and hand-stitched on the back of the quilt. More ornate labels can be computer printed or include piecing, appliqué or photo transfers. Don't forget this vital part of your quilt.

CHAPTER 2

QUILTS

Whether you have "researched" or "jumped" to get to this section, this is the playground of the book. No matter the extent of your knowledge or lack of it, you will learn the most from "doing" and this portion of the book devoted to "doing."

Bright or subdued, large or small, simple or more complex, traditional or artistic, there are a variety of quilting projects to tempt you. The quilts are divided by the types of serging stitches used in making them.

The overlock stitch is a commonly used stitch and an easy step into making your first serged quilt. Choose from a quilted wallhanging (*Spinning Pinwheels*), a baby quilt (*Playtime*) or larger quilts.

With a little fabric folding and turning a few dials, you can serge creative flatlock stitches. Use your flatlock stitching to make pieced or appliquéd quilts such as *Simply Leafy* or *Sing the Harmonies*.

Your serger's ability to make rolled edges not only serves to finish napkins and ruffled dresses; you can also create a garden of blooming quilts, such as *Garden Arbor* and *Arbor Awnings*.

To complete the picture, you can combine serging techniques in artworks for your walls like *Down the Pathway* or, as in the case of the sassy little "*Look at Me*" handbag, "art-to-go."

Whether practicing or perfecting your skills, put your serger to work and enjoy the "doing."

SPINNING PINWHEELS

When spring winds blow and new flowers grow, catch the action with a spinning pinwheel quilt. Two coordinating fabrics combine to make three-dimensional pinwheels that pop off the surface. This easy quilt is made from four fat quarters and has just a touch of serging to start you practicing your serging skills.

Serger skills include: Wide overlock stitch, using decorative thread in upper loopers

Finished size: 21" × 21"

Fabric	Cut	Into	For
Cream No. 1	2 squares, 10" × 10", crosscut	4 quarter-square triangles	Blocks
	3 strips, 2" × width of fat quarter		Binding
Cream No. 2	2 squares, 10" × 10", crosscut	4 quarter-square triangles	Blocks
	2 strips, 2" × **WOFQ**		Binding
Purple print	4 strips, 2¼" × **WOFQ**	16 rectangles, 2½" × 4½"	Pinwheels
	3 strips, 2¼" × **WOFQ**	22 squares, 2¼" × 2¼"	Borders
Purple solid	4 strips, 2¼" × **WOFQ**	16 rectangles, 2½" × 4½"	Pinwheels
	3 strips, 2¼" × **WOFQ**	22 squares, 2¼" × 2¼"	Borders

Serger Setup:

Overlock Stitch	Left Needle	Right Needle	Upper Looper	Lower Looper	Stitch Length	Stitch Width	Stitch Finger
Wide	N	—	N	N	N	N	N

Serger Threading:

Left Needle	Right Needle	Upper Looper	Lower Looper
50 wt purple cotton or polyester	—	Variegated color metallic	50 wt purple cotton or polyester

Materials

Fat quarter cream No. 1 (block background, binding)

Fat quarter cream No. 2 (block background, binding)

Fat quarter purple print (pinwheels, borders)

Fat quarter purple solid (pinwheels, borders)

2 spools purple thread (serging)

Variegated metallic thread (serging)

Neutral sewing thread

24" × 24" batting

1 yd. backing fabric and rod pocket

4 medium beads in a matching color

48 small beads in a coordinating color

Basic serging and quilting tools and supplies

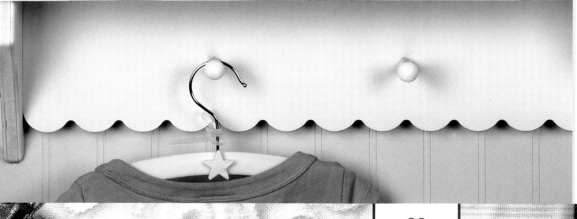

CONSTRUCT

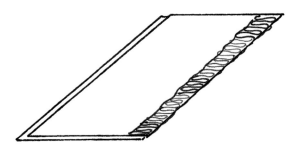

NOTES FROM NANCY

To add additional interest to the pinwheel design, select two coordinating colors of decorative thread, using one color for the upper looper and the second for the lower looper. Since the fabric is folded in the finished design, both thread colors will be featured!

1: Set up your serger for a wide three-thread overlock stitch. Refer to *Practicing Stitches–Overlock Stitch* (pages 14–15) for additional information on this stitch.

2: With wrong sides together, match the purple solid rectangles with the purple print rectangles. Place the purple solid side up and the purple print facing the bed of the machine. Serge an overlock stitch on a 4½" side of each set of rectangles.

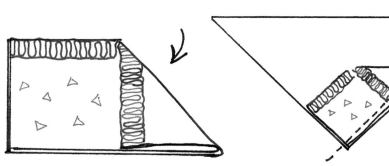

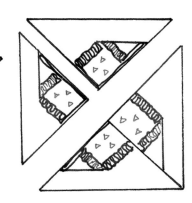

3: To form pinwheels, fold the right serged corner down to the bottom raw edge as shown. Make 8 print pinwheels with the solid corner folded down and 8 solid pinwheels with the print corner folded down. Press.

4: Place the 8 print pinwheels on the right side of background no. 1. Pin the pinwheels to the short sides of the 8 cream triangles as shown. Baste in place.

5: Lay out the block. With right sides together, machine-stitch the triangles into a diagonal four patch. Make 2 blocks.

6: Repeat with background no. 2 and the solid pinwheels creating the pinwheels as you stitch the block. Make 2 blocks.

Tip

Pressing test: Before pressing on your pinwheel blocks, test the iron temperature by pressing a test sample

of your metallic thread. High temperatures may damage your thread. Lower the iron temperature, use a press

cloth and avoid pressing directly on the thread to prevent possible thread damage.

ASSEMBLE

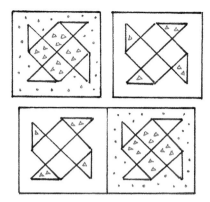

1: Lay out the 4 blocks, alternating background colors. Stitch together.

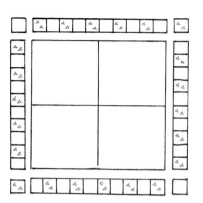

2: Lay out the border squares around the quilt center. Start with a solid square in the upper left corner and alternate the solid and print squares around the quilt. You will have a solid square in the upper left corner and lower right corner and a print square in the upper right and lower left corner.

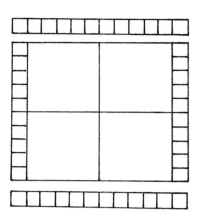

3: Stitch the side squares together and add to the sides of the quilt. Stitch the top and bottom borders together and add to the quilt.

QUILT AND FINISH

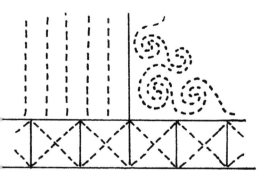

1: Layer the quilt top, batting and backing. Baste for quilting. Quilt swirls in 2 blocks and quilt vertical lines in the 2 alternating blocks. Lift the pinwheels to avoid catching them in the quilting. Crosshatch the border blocks.

2: Stitch the binding strips together with diagonal seams. Alternate the 2 background fabrics. Press in half lengthwise with the right side of the fabric showing. Bind the quilt with a continuous binding. Refer to *Reviewing Quilting Terms & Techniques—Continuous Binding* (pages 21–22) for further instruction.

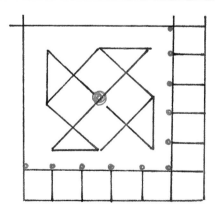

3: Hand-stitch a medium bead to the center of each pinwheel. Stitch small beads around the border of the quilt.

4: Add a rod pocket and a label to the back of the quilt.

THIRTEEN'S A CHARM

Thirteen is a charm when you combine thirteen bright and colorful fabrics into an eye-catching quilt. This is a fabulous quilt to start merging your serging into quilting. A basic serger overlock stitch is used to join fabric strips. These strip sets are recut and serged into half-square triangle blocks. Thirteen's a Charm has the appeal of an old-fashioned scrap quilt complete with prairie points, but made with speedy serging.

Serger skills include: Narrow overlock stitch, wide overlock stitch, threading, and disengaging the cutting blade

Finished size: 56" × 80"

Fabric	Cut	Into	For
Blue check	1 strip, 7½" × width of fabric	3 squares, 7½" × 7½"	Blocks
	1 strip, 8" × WOF	2 squares, 8" × 8", cut diagonally into 4 half-square triangles	Pieced blocks
		3 squares 4" × 4"	Prairie points
	5 strips, 2" × WOF		Binding
	Remainder of fabric for strata sets		Pieced blocks
All other fabrics	Cut from each of the 12 fabrics		
	1 strip, 7½" × WOF	3 squares, 7½" × 7½" (cut 4 from green/blue plaid)	Blocks
	1 strip, 8" × WOF	2 squares, 8" × 8", cut diagonally into 4 half-square triangles	Pieced blocks
		3 squares 4" × 4"	Prairie points
	Remainder of fabric for strata sets*		Pieced blocks
Backing	2 rectangles, 90" × WOF	2 lengthwise strips 2" × 60"	Facings
		Piece remainder lengthwise	Quilt back

*Strata sets: You will need 10 sets of strips; 5 combinations of fabrics cut to the measurements of set A and 5 combinations of fabrics cut to the measurements of set B. Vary the colors in each combination and the placement of the colors.
{Set A: Cut strips 1¼", 1¾", 1¾", 2¼" × WOF}   {Set B: Cut strips 1¾", 2", 1¼", 2" × WOF}

Serger Setup:

Overlock Stitch	Left Needle	Right Needle	Upper Looper	Lower Looper	Stitch Length	Stitch Width	Stitch Finger
3-thread narrow	—	N	N	N	N	N	N
3-thread wide	N	—	N	N	N	N	N

Serger Threading:

Left Needle	Right Needle	Upper Looper	Lower Looper
—	40 wt dark brown cotton*	40 wt dark brown cotton*	40 wt dark brown cotton*

*For extra practice in threading your serger, coordinate the thread colors with your fabric colors when serging strips. I used three thread colors: red, blue and brown. Serge the coordinating thread on strips in all the sets, change thread color and serge the remaining strips with the second and third thread colors.

Materials

1⅛ yd. blue check (blocks, prairie points, binding)

⅞ yd. blue ribbons (blocks, prairie points)

⅞ yd. red floral (blocks, prairie points)

⅞ yd. red print (blocks, prairie points)

⅞ yd. orange geometric (blocks, prairie points)

⅞ yd. yellow floral (blocks, prairie points)

⅞ yd. yellow ribbons (blocks, prairie points)

⅞ yd. green ribbons (blocks, prairie points)

⅞ yd. green print (blocks, prairie points)

⅞ yd. green stripe (blocks, prairie points)

⅞ yd. green/blue plaid (blocks, prairie points)

⅞ yd. brown/blue dots (blocks, prairie points)

⅞ yd. brown multicolored print (blocks, prairie points)

3 spools brown serging thread

*optional—3 spools of red serging thread

*optional—3 spools of blue serging thread

60" × 84" batting

5 yd. backing (quilt back, facings)

9" or larger square ruler

Basic serging and quilting tools and supplies

CONSTRUCT

PIECED BLOCKS

SET A

1¼"	
1¾"	
1¾"	
2¼"	

SET B

1¾"	
2"	
1¼"	
2"	

1: Set up your serger for a narrow three-thread overlock stitch by removing the left needle and serging only with the right needle. Your serged seam should be slightly less than ¼". Refer to *Practicing Stitches–Overlock Stitch* (page 15) for additional information on this stitch.

2: With wrong sides together, overlock stitch the strips of Set A strata. The serging stitches and seam allowances will be showing on the right side of the fabrics. Press the seams to one side so the upper looper thread is visible.

3: With wrong sides together, overlock stitch the strips of Set B strata. Again, the serging stitches will be on the right side of the fabrics. Press the seams to one side so the upper looper thread is visible.

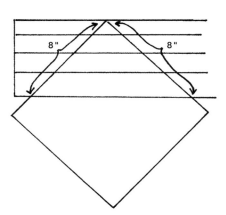

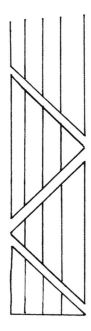

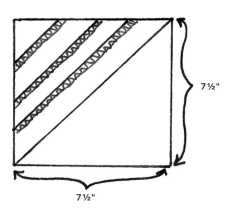

4: Using a square ruler, cut 45-degree triangles from the strata sets. When you set your ruler with zero at the top of the fabric, the sides should be 8" long. Use masking tape to mark your ruler for easy reference when cutting the remaining triangles.

5: Alternate cutting the strata triangles so fabric strip A1 (or B1) is at the top of triangle 1, the bottom of triangle 2, and the top of triangle 3, etc. Cut 5 triangles from each strip set for a total of 50 triangles. (You will only use 48 of the triangles.)

6: Match each strata triangle with a half-square triangle. With the right sides together, serge or machine-stitch to form 48 square blocks. (You will have 2 half-square triangles that will not be used.) Press seam allowances toward the half-square triangle. Square the blocks by trimming to 7½" × 7½". Refer to *Quilting Terms & Techniques–Squaring Half-Square Triangle Blocks* (page 20) for additional information on trimming blocks.

PRAIRIE POINTS

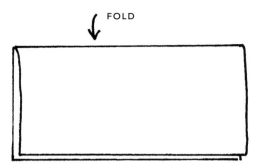

1: Fold the 4 squares in half with wrong sides together. Press.

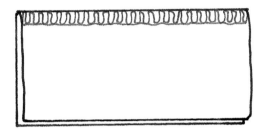

2: Disengage the serger cutting blade. Serge the folded edge of each square. Sew carefully along the edge so the serged thread lies on the fold and the fabric does not roll under.

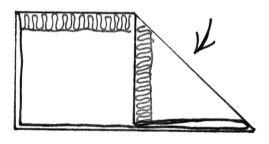

3: To fold a prairie point, keep the folded edge on top with the lower looper thread facing you. Fold the right corner to the center.

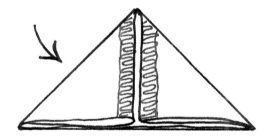

4: Fold the left corner to the center. All of the raw edges should now be on the bottom and the upper looper thread should be showing and running down the center of the prairie point. Press. Baste along the bottom raw edges of the prairie points. Make 32 prairie points. (You will have 4 extra 4" squares.)

To give narrow strips of fabric extra support, spray the strips with spray starch and iron before serging. You'll be pleased how this simple step can improve the serging experience!

ASSEMBLE

In the DVD, Sharon and I feature her *Thirteen's A Charm* quilt in great detail. Be certain to view this segment—and all the others too—to appreciate all the details of this unique quilt design!

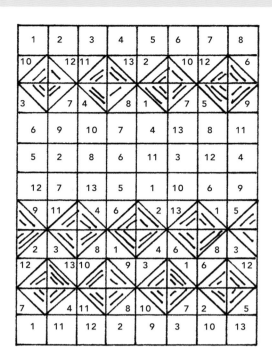

1: Re-engage your cutting blades. Set up your serger for a wide overlock stitch by removing the right needle and placing it in the left needle position.

2: Lay out your blocks, arranging the blocks so you have a pleasing combination of colors and fabric patterns.

Suggested combination: (1) red floral; (2) brown/blue dots; (3) red print; (4) brown multicolored print; (5) green print; (6) green/blue plaid; (7) orange geometric; (8) blue check; (9) yellow ribbons; (10) green ribbons; (11) green stripe; (12) blue ribbons; (13) yellow floral

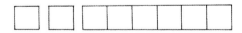

3: With right sides together, serge or machine-stitch the blocks into horizontal rows.

4: With wrong sides together, serge the plain block rows to the triangle rows. The serging will be showing on the right side of the quilt top.

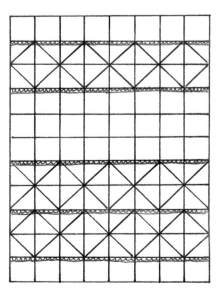

5: With right sides together, serge or machine-stitch the remaining rows together completing the quilt top as indicated in the diagram.

QUILT AND FINISH

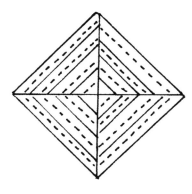

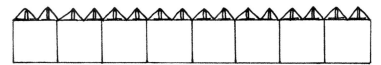

1: Layer the quilt top, batting and backing. Baste for quilting. Quilt random straight lines in the pieced triangles. Quilt a scalloped cable across the plain blocks.

2: Lay out 16 prairie points on the top of the quilt, varying colors and fabric designs. Evenly space so there are two prairie points on each of the 8 blocks. Repeat for the bottom of the quilt.

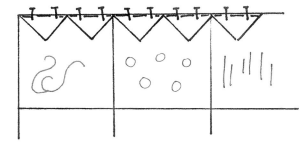

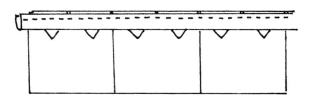

3: With the right side of the quilt matching the serged side of the prairie point, pin the prairie points to the quilt edge. Keep the raw edges even. Repeat for the bottom of the quilt.

4: With wrong sides together, press the 2" strips of facing fabric in half lengthwise making a 1" facing. Stitch the folded facing to the top of the quilt catching in the prairie points. Press the seam allowances toward the facing. Trim the facing even with the quilt sides.

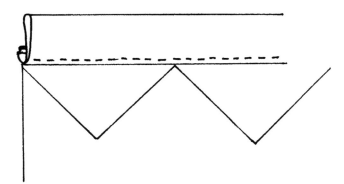

5: Machine-stitch close to the seamed edge of the facing only stitching through the facing and the seam allowances. (This understitching technique is often used in garment construction to help facings lie flat.)

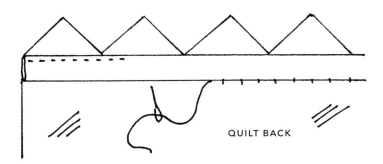

QUILT BACK

6: Press the facing to the back of the quilt. Hand-stitch the lower edge of the facing to the back of the quilt. Be careful so your stitches do not go through to the front of the quilt. Repeat the steps to add facing to the bottom of the quilt.

7: Piece the 2" binding strips with diagonal seams. Press in half lengthwise. Bind the sides of the quilt. Refer to *Quilting Terms & Techniques–Binding with Overlapped Corners*, steps 4–6 (page 23) for further instruction.

8: Add a label to the back of the quilt.

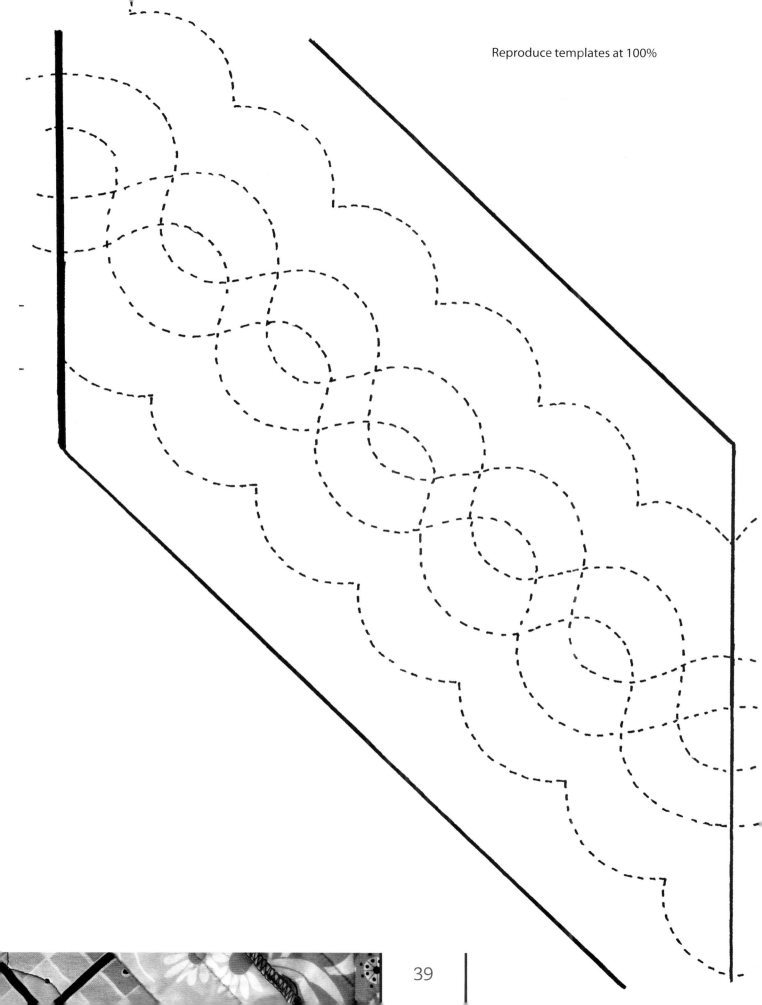

PLAYTIME

Tumble into playtime with a nostalgic juvenile print. You can pile four patch blocks just as a child piles building blocks. Use overlock stitched serging as a decorative touch as you put blocks together with seams showing, not hidden on the back of the quilt top.

Serger skills include: Wide overlock stitch, changing threads

Finished size: 48" × 56"

Fabric	Cut	For
Turquoise	2 lengthwise strips, 4½" × 48½"	Borders—side
	2 lengthwise strips, 4½" × 40½"	Borders—top/bottom
	7 lengthwise strips, 2½" × 42"	Four Patches
Print	6 squares, 8½" × 8½"	Plain blocks
	3 rectangles, 8½" × 16½"	Rectangular blocks
	2 strips, 2½" × WOF	Four patches
	1 strip, 2½" × WOF	Border corners
Brown	2 strips, 2½" × WOF	Four patches
	6 strips, 2" × WOF	Binding
Red	2 strips, 4½" × WOF	Large four patches
	1 strip, 2½" × WOF	Border corners
Gold	2 strips, 4½" × WOF	Large four patches
Pink	3 strips, 2½" × WOF	Four patches

Serger Setup:

Overlock Stitch	Left Needle	Right Needle	Upper Looper	Lower Looper	Stitch Length	Stitch Width	Stitch Finger
3-thread wide	N	—	N	N	N	N	N

Serger Threading:

	Left Needle	Right Needle	Upper Looper	Lower Looper
Pink/turquoise four patches	50 wt pink cotton	—	50 wt pink cotton	50 wt pink cotton
Red/gold four patches	50 wt red cotton	—	50 wt red cotton	50 wt red cotton
Red/print four patches	50 wt red cotton	—	50 wt red cotton	50 wt red cotton

Materials

1½ yd. turquoise (four patches, borders)

1⅛ yd. juvenile print (four patches, plain blocks, border corners)

¾ yd. brown (four patches, binding)

½ yd. red (large four patches, border corners)

½ yd. gold (large four patches)

⅓ yd. pink (four patches)

3 spools pink 50 wt cotton thread (serging)

3 spools red 50 wt cotton thread (serging)

52" × 60" batting

3 yd. backing

Basic sewing tools and supplies

CONSTRUCT

PINK/TURQUOISE FOUR PATCHES (MAKE 24)

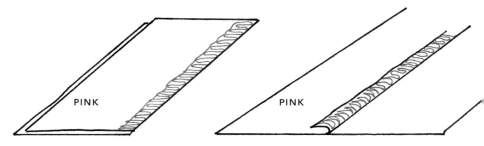

1: Set up your serger for a wide overlock stitch. Refer to *Practicing Stitches–Overlock Stitch* (pages 14–15) for additional information on this stitch.

2: Place pink and turquoise strips wrong sides together and serge with pink thread in the loopers. Place the pink strip on top and the turquoise strip on the bed of the serger when stitching. The seams will be on the right side of the fabrics. Stitch 3 sets of strips.

3: Press the seam toward the pink strip, revealing the pink lower looper thread on the surface.

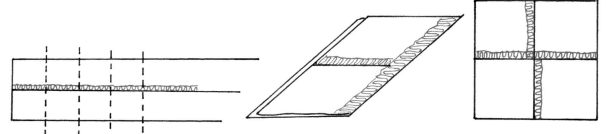

4: Recut the strips into 48 2½" units.

5: Place the units wrong sides together, rotating one unit so like colors are opposite each other, and serge into units of 4 squares, or "four patches."

6: Press to one side showing the lower looper thread on the surface.

BROWN/TURQUOISE FOUR PATCHES (MAKE 16)

1: Place the brown and turquoise strips right sides together and serge or machine-stitch. Press the seam toward the brown strip. The seams will be on the wrong sides of the fabrics. Stitch 2 sets of strips.

2: Recut the strips into 32 2½" units.

3: Place the units right sides together, rotating one unit so the like colors are opposite each other and serge or stitch into four patches.

4: Press the seam allowance to one side.

PRINT/TURQUOISE FOUR PATCHES (MAKE 12)

1: Place the print and turquoise strips right sides together and serge or machine-stitch. Press the seam toward the print strip. The seams will be on the wrong sides of the fabrics. Stitch 2 sets of strips.

2: Recut the strips into 24 2½" units.

3: Place the units right sides together, rotating one unit so the like colors are opposite each other, and serge or stitch into four patches.

4: Press the seam allowances to one side.

RED/GOLD LARGE FOUR PATCHES (MAKE 5)

1: Place the red and gold strips wrong sides together and serge with red thread in the loopers. Place the red strip on top when serging. The seams will be on the right side of the fabrics. Stitch 2 sets of strips.

2: Press toward the red strip revealing the red lower looper thread on the surface.

3: Recut the strips into 10 4½" units.

4: Place the units wrong sides together, rotating one unit so the like colors are opposite each other, and serge into four patches.

5: Press the seam allowances to one side, revealing the red lower looper thread.

RED/PRINT CORNER FOUR PATCHES (MAKE 4)

1: Place the red and print strips wrong sides together and serge with red thread in the loopers. Place the red strip on top when serging. The seams will be on the right side of the fabrics. Stitch 1 strip.

2: Press toward the red strip, revealing the red lower looper thread on the surface.

3: Recut the strips into 8 2½" units.

4: Place the units wrong sides together, rotating one unit so the like colors are opposite each other, and serge into four patches.

5: Press the seam allowances to one side, revealing the red lower looper thread.

ASSEMBLE

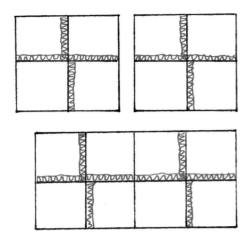

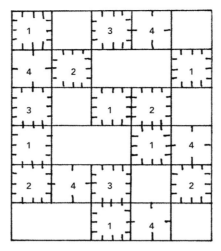

1: With right sides together, serge or machine-stitch the matching four patches into 16 patch blocks. Press the seam allowances to one side. Make 6 pink/turquoise blocks. Make 4 brown/turquoise blocks. Make 3 print/turquoise blocks.

2: Lay out the 16 patch blocks, the large red/gold four patch blocks and the plain blocks. A suggested layout is shown: (1) pink/turquoise, (2) brown/turquoise, (3) print/turquoise, (4) red/gold. With right sides together, serge or stitch the blocks into rows. With right sides together, serge or stitch the rows together, completing the center of the quilt top.

3: With right sides together, add the turquoise side borders.

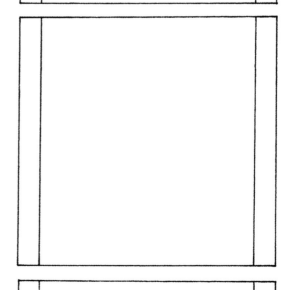

4: With right sides together, add a small red/print four patch to each end on the top and bottom borders.

5: With right sides together, add the top and bottom borders to the quilt.

QUILT AND FINISH

1: Layer the quilt top, batting and backing. Baste for quilting.

2: Stitch diagonal lines from corner to corner to crosshatch the quilt center. Quilt elephants in the turquoise border surrounded by straight lines. Crosshatch the border corners.

3: Stitch the binding strips together with diagonal seams. Press in half lengthwise with wrong sides together. Bind the quilt with a continuous binding. Refer to *Quilting Terms & Techniques—Continuous Binding* (pages 21–22) for further instruction.

4: To complete the quilt, add a rod pocket and label.

Reproduce templates at 100%

ALICE'S FLOWER GARDEN

When Alice stepped into an enchanted world, she found herself in a flower garden of giant blooms connected with strands of gold. You may choose only the basic colors for your quilt, or you may imitate Mother Nature and select several shades and prints of each color. Even though you may use slightly more fabric, you will add sparkle and interest to your quilt.

Serger skills include: Wide overlock stitch

Finished size: 93" × 103"

Fabric	Cut	Into	For
Cream	16 strips, 4" × WOF	76 half hexagons*	Background
	4 strips, 4" × WOF	26 diamonds*	Background
	2 strips, 4" × WOF	26 triangle A (equilateral triangles)*	Background
	2 strips, 2¾" × WOF	12 triangle B (edge triangles)*	Background
	3 strips, 2¾" × WOF	12 triangle C (corner triangles)*	Background
		12 triangle C reversed (corner triangles)*	Background
Red	15 strips, 4" × WOF	72 half hexagons*	Flowers
	3 strips, 4" × WOF	17 diamonds*	Flowers
	2 strips, 4" × WOF	17 triangle A (equilateral triangles)*	Flowers
Blue	12 strips, 4" × WOF	56 half hexagons*	Flowers
	3 strips, 4" × WOF	19 diamonds*	Flowers
	2 strips, 4" × WOF	19 triangle A (equilateral triangles)*	Flowers
Green A	11 strips, 4" × WOF	52 half hexagons*	Leaves
	2 strips, 4" × WOF	12 diamonds*	Leaves
	1 strip, 4" × WOF	12 triangle A (equilateral triangles)*	Leaves
Yellow	4 strips, 4" × WOF	20 half hexagons*	Flower Centers
	2 strips, 4" × WOF	10 diamonds*	Flower Centers
	1 strip, 4" × WOF	10 triangle A (equilateral triangles)*	Flower Centers
	10 strips, 1" × WOF		Folded Trim
Green B– 96" wide	1 backing, 108" × WOF		Backing
	4 strips, 5½" × WOF		Borders
	5 strips, 2" × WOF		Binding
or Green B– 42" wide	1 strip, 108" × WOF		Backing Center
	2 strips, 108" × WOF	2 lengthwise strips, 28" wide × 108" long	Backing Sides
		4 lengthwise strips, 5½" wide × 108" long	Borders
	12 strips, 2" × WOF		Binding

Serger Setup:

Overlock Stitch	Left Needle	Right Needle	Upper Looper	Lower Length	Stitch Length	Stitch Width	Stitch Finger
Wide	N	—	N	N	N	N	N

Serger Threading:

Left Needle	Right Needle	Upper Looper	Lower Looper
50 wt gold cotton	—	40 wt variegated gold	40 wt variegated gold

Materials

3 yd. cream
(background)

2½ yd. red
(flowers)

2⅛ yd. blue
(flowers)

1¾ yd. green
A (leaves)

1⅓ yd. yellow
(flower centers,
folded trim)

4¼ yd. green
B–96" wide fabric
(borders, binding,
backing)

or 10 yd. green
B–42 wide fabric
(borders, binding,
backing)

2 spools 40
wt variegated
gold thread

50 wt gold
thread

96" × 108"
batting

Basic serging and
quilting tools
and supplies

* Pattern pieces
included on
pages 51–52.
Open strips and
lay the corre-
sponding pattern
piece on the
strip. Trim to size.
Alternate placing
the base of the
half hexagon
and the triangles
on the top and
bottom of the
strip for more
efficient use of
the fabric.

ASSEMBLE

1: Set up your serger for a wide three-thread overlock stitch. Refer to *Practicing Stitches–Overlock Stitch* (page 15) for additional information on this stitch.

2: Lay out your half hexagons, diamonds and triangles following the quilt layout.

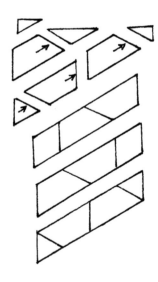

3: With right sides together, machine-stitch or serge the pieces into the rows of section 1.

4: With wrong sides together, overlock stitch the first and second full rows of section 1. The serging will be on the right side of the fabrics. With right sides together, overlock stitch the second and third full rows of section one. The serging will be on the wrong sides of the fabrics. Continue alternating so the serging is on the right side of every second row as shown.

5: Repeat to stitch together the pieces and rows of sections 2–6.

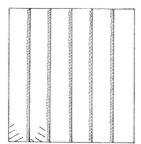

6: With wrong sides together, serge the sections together to complete the quilt top.

7: Piece 5 of the yellow 1" strips with diagonal seams. With wrong sides together, press the strips in half lengthwise to form ½" folded trim pieces. Make 2.

8: On the right side of the quilt top and with raw edges even, machine-baste the 2 folded trim strips to the sides of the quilt top. Trim to fit. With raw edges even, machine-baste the remainder of the trim strips to the top and bottom of the quilt top. Trim border strips to fit.

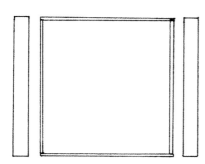

9: With right sides together, serge or machine-stitch 2 5½" border strips to the sides of the quilt top, catching in the folded trim. Trim to fit. Press seams toward the borders.

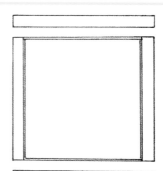

10: With right sides together, serge or machine-stitch the 2 remaining 5½" borders to the top and bottom of the quilt top. Catch the folded trim in the stitching. Trim border strips to fit. Press seams toward the borders.

QUILT AND FINISH

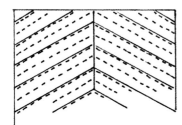

1: Layer the quilt top, batting and backing. Baste for quilting. Quilt down all the visible overlock stitched seams. Using gold thread, stitch in the ditch and midlines following the diagonal lines formed by the serged seams.

2: Quilt large free-form leaves on the borders.

3: Piece the 2 binding strips with diagonal seams. Press in half lengthwise. Bind the quilt with a continuous binding. Refer to *Quilting Terms & Techniques—Continuous Binding* (pages 21–22) for further instruction.)

4: Add a label to the back of the quilt.

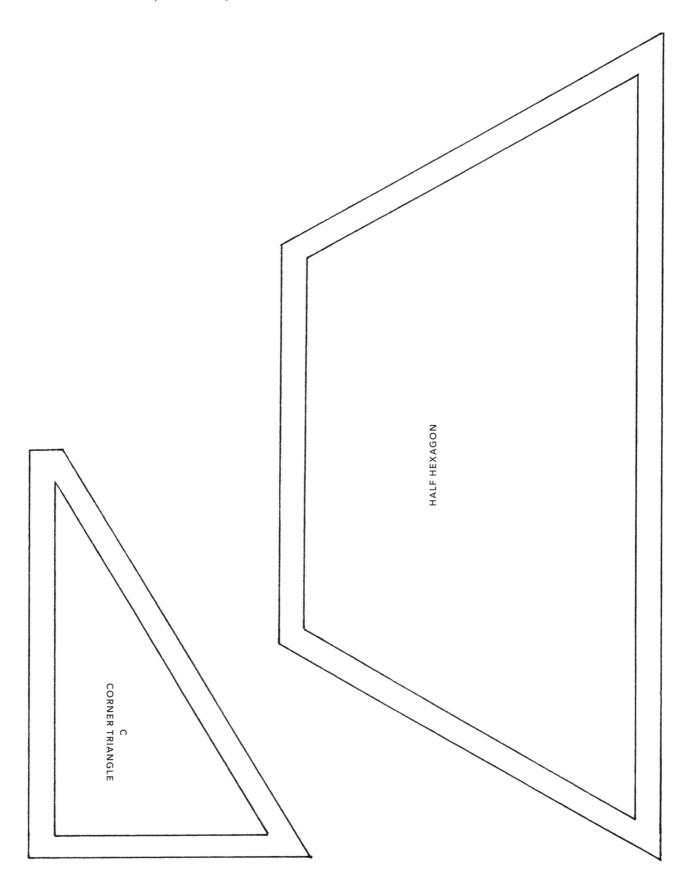

HALF HEXAGON

C
CORNER TRIANGLE

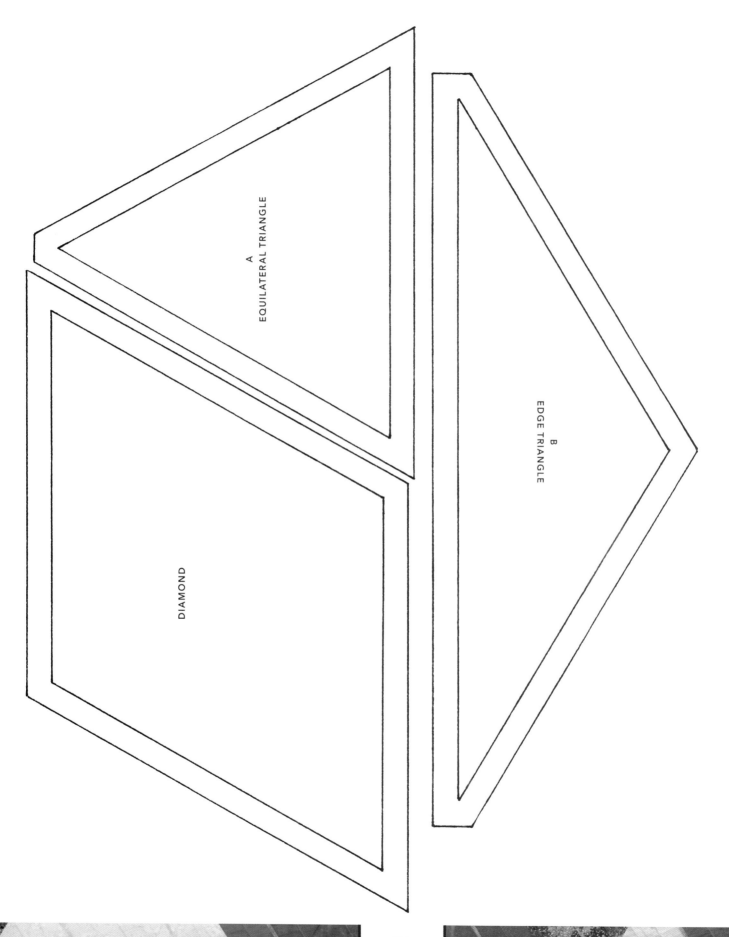

A
EQUILATERAL TRIANGLE

B
EDGE TRIANGLE

DIAMOND

51

MIXED BOUQUET

Collect a mixed bouquet of your favorite floral fabrics and combine them in this quilt. The entire quilt is serged, right to the quilting step, giving you a wonderful chance to use your serging skills. Finish your quilt with a romantic scalloped edge…serged, of course.

Serger skill included: Overlock stitching

Finished size: 44" × 54"

Fabric	Cut	Into	For
Med/dark green	2 strips, 2" × WOF	8 rectangles, 2" × 9"	Sashing
	3 strips, 2" × WOF	3 rectangles, 2" × 29½"*	Sashing
	4 strips, 3½" × WOF	2 rectangles, 3½ × 40"*	Inner border
		2 rectangles, 3½ × 35½"*	Inner border
	12 flower baskets using pattern		Blocks
Floral prints (cut from each of 6)	2 squares, 9" × 9"		Blocks
	5 scallops using template		Scallops
Green leaf print	5 strips, 1½" × WOF		Outer border
Backing	1 rectangle, 54" × WOF		Quilt back
	30 scallops using pattern		Scallops back

*Due to variations in serging, check your quilt's measurements and trim length accordingly.

Serger Setup:

Overlock Stitch	Left Needle	Right Needle	Upper Looper	Lower Looper	Stitch Length	Stitch Width	Stitch Finger
3-thread - Wide (green metallic)	N	—	3	6	N	N	N
3-thread - Wide (gold cotton)	N	—	N	N	N	N	N

Serger Threading:

Overlock Stitch	Left Needle	Right Needle	Upper Looper	Lower Looper
Flower Baskets	Green serging thread	—	Green metallic	Green serging thread
Sashing, borders, scallops	50 wt gold cotton	—	50 wt gold cotton	50 wt gold cotton

Materials

1¼ yd. tone-on-tone medium/dark green (sashing, inner border)

6 fat quarters of different floral prints (blocks, scallops)

⅜ yd. green leaf print (outer border)

3 spools of gold 50 wt cotton thread

Green metallic thread

2 spools of green serging thread

54" × 64" batting

2⅜ yd. backing and a rod pocket

Template plastic

Fabric glue stick

Basic serging and quilting tools and supplies

CONSTRUCT

Many sergers have an adjustable differential feed feature that changes the speed of the front feed dogs. When serging around corners or curves, consider adjusting the differential feed lever to a plus number to ease the scalloped edge. This slight change will prevent the curve from bowing out of shape. As with all changes, test on a scrap of fabric to determine the best serger setting.

1: Set up your serger for a wide three-thread overlock stitch with green metallic thread. Refer to *Practicing Stitches—Overlock Stitch* (page 15) for additional information on this stitch.

2: Overlock stitch the curved edge of the flower basket. Place the fabric right side up on the serger so the metallic thread is seen. Make 12.

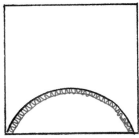

3: Place a flower basket on the lower edge of each of the 12 floral blocks. Hand-baste or use a fabric glue stick to baste the serged flower baskets to the blocks.

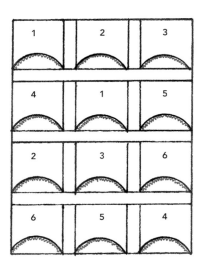

4: Lay out the blocks and sashing strips. Distribute the 6 floral fabrics as shown.

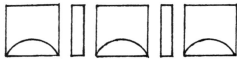

5: Set up the serger with the gold thread in the upper looper. With wrong sides together, overlock stitch the blocks and sashing of the top row. To have a consistent look to the serging, serge with the green sashing strip on top and the floral block facing the bed of the serger. Repeat for the remaining rows.

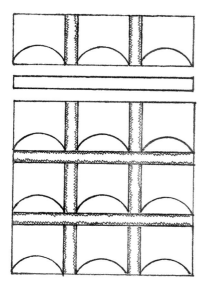

6: With wrong sides together, overlock stitch the sashing between the rows. Serge with the green sashing strip on top and the blocks facing the bed of the serger. Serge the rows together completing the center of the quilt.

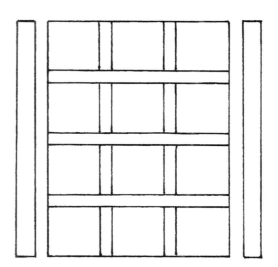

7: Measure the length of the sides of the quilt for the inner side borders. If needed, trim the two 40" medium/dark green inner border rectangles to the correct length. With wrong sides together, serge the inner side borders to the quilt top. Again, place the green border strip on top under the serger. Press.

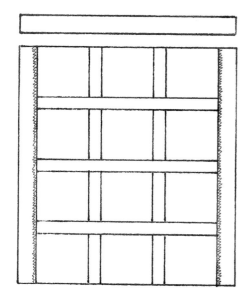

8: Measure across the quilt top and the two side borders for the correct length needed for the top and bottom inner borders. Trim the two 35½" medium/dark green inner border rectangles to the needed length. With wrong sides together, serge the inner top and bottom borders to the quilt. Place the green side on top under the serger. Press.

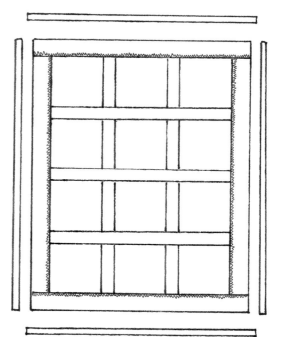

9: Inconspicuously, piece the 1½" green print outer border strips. Measure the quilt for the length needed for the outer side borders. Cut two side border strips from the pieced strips. With right sides together, serge the outer side borders to the quilt. Repeat for the outer top and bottom borders.

QUILT AND FINISH

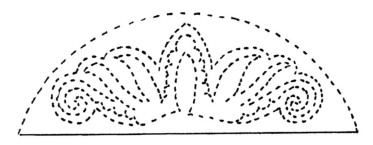

1: Layer the quilt top, batting and backing for quilting.

2: Quilt along the curved edge of the floral baskets. Use the quilting design to quilt the floral baskets.

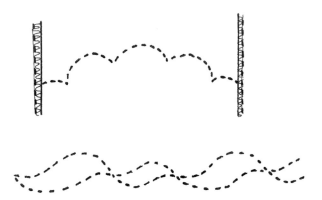

3: Quilt down all the exposed serged seams. Quilt a wavy design in the sashing and borders. Use the scalloped quilting guide to quilt the blocks.

4: Trim away the excess batting and backing.

SCALLOPS

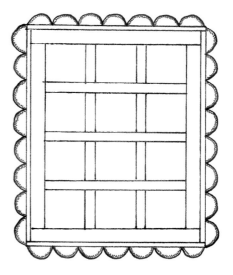

1: Use the pattern piece to trace the scallop on the right side of the floral fabrics. Make 30.

2: Layer with batting and backing. With the right side up on the serger, serge the curved edge, trimming off ¼" of the scallop, batting and backing.

3: Lay out the scallops around the quilt. Place eight scallops on the sides of the quilt. Place seven scallops on the top and bottom of the quilt.

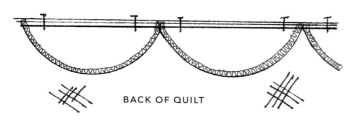

BACK OF QUILT

4: With raw edges even, pin the scallops to the back of the quilt. Overlap scallops as needed.

5: Overlock stitch the scallops to the quilt. Serge with the scallop side up.

FRONT OF QUILT

6: Press the serging and the scallops to the front of the quilt. Edge-stitch the serged stitching to the outer border completing the quilt.

7: Hand-stitch a rod pocket and a label to the back of the quilt.

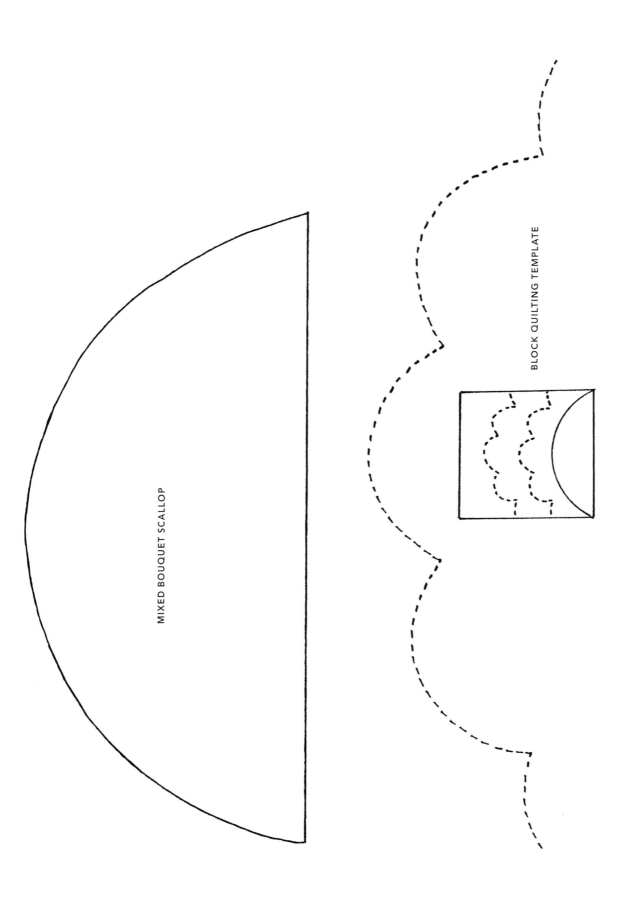

MIXED BOUQUET SCALLOP

BLOCK QUILTING TEMPLATE

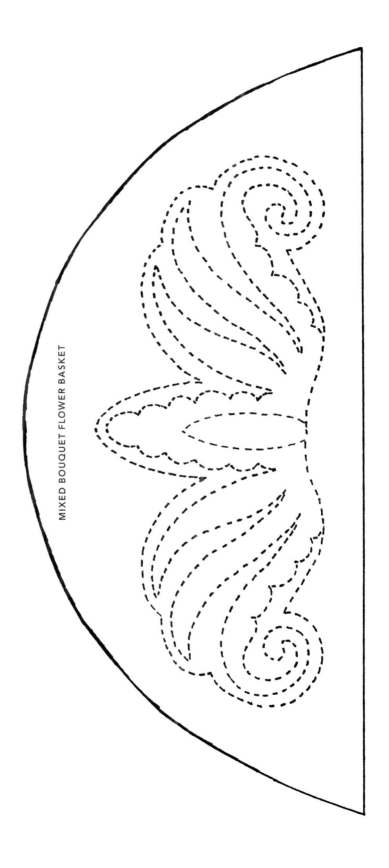

MIXED BOUQUET FLOWER BASKET

SIMPLY LEAFY

There is sleek simplicity in this two-color Simply Leafy quilt. The square is stretched into a long, slender and sophisticated rectangle. Eco-friendly fabrics, made of bamboo and organic cotton, are set off by flatlock stitching. Choose a variegated tan thread to add visual dimension to your quilt. (Don't tell a soul but that variegated thread also helps to hide any inconsistency in the stitching.)

Serger skills include: Narrow and wide two-thread flatlock stitch

Finished Size: 18" × 45"

Fabric	Cut	Into	For
Brown leaf print	2 strips, 9½" × WOF 1 strip, 3½" × WOF 4 strips, 2" × WOF	7 rectangles, 6½" × 9½" 12 rectangles, 2½" × 3½"	Blocks 9 patch blocks Binding
White	1 rectangle, 12" wide × length of fabric From the remaining fabric	9 patch blocks 5 rectangles, 6-½" x 9-½"	Blocks

Serger Setup:

Flatlock	Left Needle	Right Needle	Upper Looper	Lower Looper	Stitch Length	Stitch Width	Stitch Finger
2-thread wide	1	—	Attach 2-thread converter	5	3.0	N	N
2-thread narrow	—	1	Attach 2-thread converter	5	3.0	N	N

Serger Threading:

Flatlock Stitch	Left Needle	Right Needle	Upper Looper	Lower Looper
Wide	40 wt. variegated tan cotton	—	—	40 wt. variegated tan cotton
Narrow	—	40 wt. variegated tan cotton	—	40 wt. variegated tan cotton

Materials

⅔ yd. white (blocks)

1 yd. brown leaf print (blocks, binding)

2 spools variegated tan cotton thread

22" × 48" batting

1½ yd. backing

Dark brown yarn

Large-eyed needle (chenille or yarn needle)

Basic serging and quilting tools and supplies

CONSTRUCT

1: Set up your serger for a narrow two-thread flatlock stitch by placing the two-thread converter on the upper looper. Consult your owner's manual for specific directions for your serger. Refer to *Practicing Stitches—Flatlock Stitch* (page 16) for additional information on this stitch.

Note: If your serger cannot be converted to stitch a two-thread flatlock, this quilt could also be made using a three-thread overlock stitch.

WRONG SIDE OF FABRIC

2: With right sides together, press a randomly placed vertical line on a white 6½" × 9½" rectangle. Stitch a flatlock stitch along the folded edge. Approximately half of the stitch width will extend beyond the fabric edge.

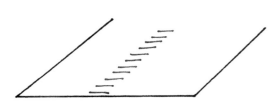

3: Open to reveal the ladder stitch on the right side of the fabric.

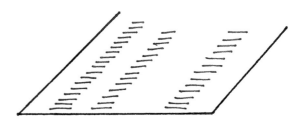

4: Randomly, press additional lines for stitching on your block. Stitch 2–3 narrow flatlock vertical rows on the block. Keep your stitching rows 1" away from the block sides to avoid interference with stitching the vertical seams. Make 7 blocks.

NOTES FROM NANCY

If your flatlock seam doesn't flatten to your liking, try guiding the fabric further away from the blade area. Part of the overlock stitch will form off the edge of the fabric, giving greater space for the fabric to expand or to lie flat. Subtle changes can really make a difference when serging!

WIDE FLATLOCK

5: For the yarn-filled rows, switch the needle to the left needle position for a wide two-thread ladder stitch. Stitch one or two wide flatlock rows on each block.

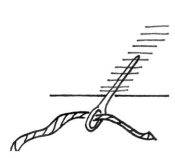

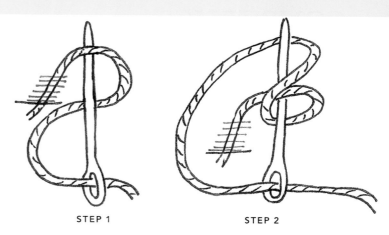

STEP 1   **STEP 2**

6: Thread a large-eyed needle with yarn. Slide the needle under the wide ladder stitches.

7: Randomly draw the thread to the surface. Make a loose knot following the steps as shown. Skip two stitches and slide the needle under the ladder stitches again.

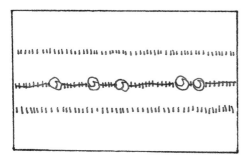

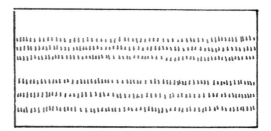

8: Continue drawing the yarn under the ladder stitches and making knots at random. Make 4–7 knots on each block.

9: With right sides together, press random vertical stitching lines on the 12" rectangle. Stitch flatlock rows using a narrow flatlock stitch. Switch to a wide flatlock for yarn-filled rows. Stitch a total of 6–7 rows.

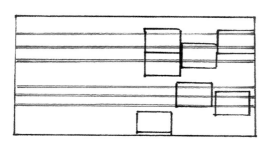

10: Cut 15 vertical blocks, 2½" × 3½" from the large serged rectangle. Vary the cutting lines so the stitching is more random. Two or three of the 15 blocks can be plain blocks cut from the remaining white fabric.

11: Draw yarn under the flatlock stitching as desired. Add knots following the same steps as for the large blocks.

ASSEMBLE

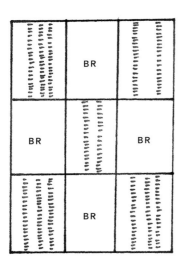

1: Lay out three 9 patch blocks using the 2½" × 3½" brown print rectangles (BR) and the ladder-stitch trimmed white rectangles.

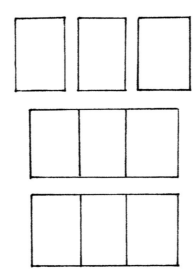

2: Stitch the rectangles into rows. Stitch the rows together forming 9 patch blocks.

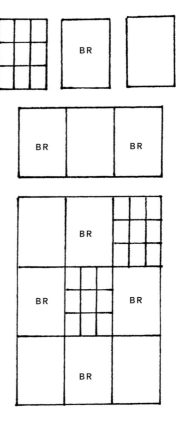

3: Using the 9 patch blocks, the 6½" × 9½" brown print rectangles (BR) and the 6½" × 9½" white rectangles, lay out the quilt top as shown. Stitch the rectangles into rows. Stitch the rows together completing the quilt top.

QUILT AND FINISH

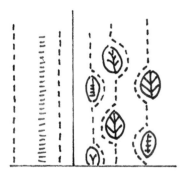

1: Layer the quilt top, batting and backing. Baste the layers together for quilting. Quilt vertical lines on the white blocks. Outline quilt the leaves in the brown print blocks.

2: Diagonally piece the 2" brown print binding strips. Press in half lengthwise with wrong sides together. Bind the quilt with a continuous binding. Refer to *Quilting Terms & Techniques—Continuous Binding* (pages 21–22) for detailed instruction.

3: Add a label and a rod pocket for hanging.

SIMPLY LEAFY 2

Graceful lines and a touch of piecing combine in this companion project to Simply Leafy. In this quilt, the long and slender look comes alive with appliqué. Use your serging skills to shadow the stems and enhance the dimensional leaves of Simply Leafy 2.

Serger skills include: Wide and narrow two-thread flatlock stitch, two-thread overlock stitch

Finished size: 12" × 27"

Fabric	Cut	Into	For
White	1 rectangle, 8½" × 27½" 1 rectangle, 10" × 27" 2 strips, 2" × **WOF**		Background Blocks Binding
Light green	4 bias strips, 1" × 26"		Appliquéd stems
Brown leaf print	1 strip, 3½" × **WOF** 1 strip, 2" × **WOF**	9 rectangles, 2½" × 3½"	Blocks Binding
Dark brown flannel	1½" strips, 3" × **WOF** Remainder used for back of leaves		Appliquéd leaves

Serger Setup:

	Left Needle	Right Needle	Upper Looper	Lower Looper	Stitch Length	Stitch Width	Stitch Finger
Two-thread flatlock Wide (Blocks)	1	—	Attach two-thread converter	5	3.0	N	N
Two-thread flatlock Narrow (Blocks)	—	1	Attach two-thread converter	5	3.0	N	N
Two-thread flatlock Narrow (Flannel)	—	2	Attach two-thread converter	6	3.0	N	N
Two-thread overlock Narrow	—	3	Attach two-thread converter	6	N	N	N

Serger Threading:

	Left Needle	Right Needle	Upper Looper	Lower Looper
Wide two-thread flatlock (blocks)	40 wt variegated tan cotton	—	—	40 wt variegated tan cotton
Narrow two-thread flatlock (blocks)	—	40 wt variegated tan cotton	—	40 wt variegated tan cotton
Narrow two-thread flatlock (leaves)	—	Bright green		Bright green
Narrow two-thread overlock (stems)	—	Bright green	—	Bright green

Materials

1 yd. white (background, blocks, binding)

¾ yd. light green (stems)

½ yd. brown leaf print (blocks, binding)

⅜ yd. dark brown flannel (leaves)

2 spools variegated tan cotton thread (serging)

2 spools bright green thread (serging)*

Dark brown yarn (trim)

Large-eyed needle (chenille or yarn needle)

16" × 32" batting

1 yd. backing, rod pocket

Basic serging and quilting tools and supplies

*Choose thread slightly darker than the green fabric for a shadow effect.

CONSTRUCT

APPLIQUÉ BACKGROUND

WRONG SIDE OF FABRIC

1: Set up your serger for a narrow two-thread flatlock stitch. Consult your owner's manual for directions. Refer to *Practicing Stitches—Flatlock Stitch* (page 16) for more information on this stitch.

2: With right sides together, randomly press a vertical line on the white 8½" × 27½" rectangle. Stitch a flatlock stitch along the folded edge. Approximately half of the stitch width will extend beyond the fabric edge.

NOTES FROM **NANCY**

When a flatlock stitch is flattened, either a ladder stitch (needle thread) or a looped stitch (looper thread) will be visible. I always had to stop and think which way to fold the fabric—right sides or wrong sides together—to yield the respective results. So, I made up this silly phrase: "It's right to use a ladder, but wrong to get looped!" Meet right sides together to achieve the ladder stitch; wrong sides together for the looped stitch.

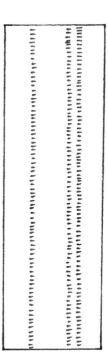

3: Pull fabric to open stitches and reveal the ladder stitch on the right side of the fabric.

4: Randomly press additional lines for flatlock stitching on your block. Stitch 3 narrow flatlock vertical rows on the block. Keep your rows 1" away from the sides to avoid interference with seaming and binding your project.

BLOCKS

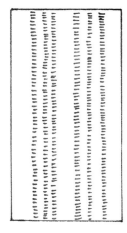 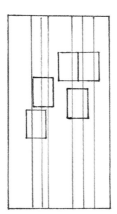 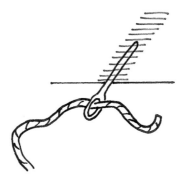

1: With right sides together, press random vertical lines on the 10" × 27" white rectangle. Stitch narrow flatlock rows. For the yarn-filled rows, switch the needle to the left needle position for a wide ladder stitch. Stitch 1 or 2 wide flatlock rows. Pull to open the ladder stitches on the right side of the fabric.

2: Cut 9 vertical rectangles 2½" × 3½" from the 10" × 27" serged white rectangle. Vary the cutting lines so the stitching is more random. Discard the remainder of the rectangle.

3: Thread a large-eyed needle with yarn. Slide the needle under the wide ladder stitches for the yarn trimmed rows.

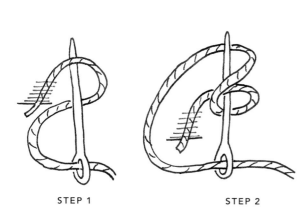

STEP 1   STEP 2

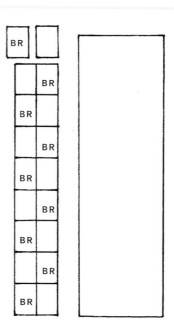

4: Randomly draw the thread to the surface. Make a loose knot following the steps as shown. Skip two stitches and slide the needle under the ladder stitches again. Make two or three knots on each block.

5: Lay out the 9 white rectangles alternating with the 9 brown leaf rectangles. Stitch together and add to the left side of the large white background rectangle.

LEAVES

1: Change to the green serger thread and again use the narrow flatlock serger stitch.

2: With right sides together, press a vertical line on the 3" brown flannel strip. Stitch a flatlock stitch along the folded edge. Approximately half of the stitch width will extend beyond the fabric edge.

3: Pull stitches open to reveal the ladder stitch on the right side of the fabric. Using the leaf pattern on page 72 as a guide, cut 11 leaves. Center each leaf on the serged line of the strip.

4: Cut 11 plain leaves from the remaining brown fabric. Make a vertical slash in the center of each plain leaf.

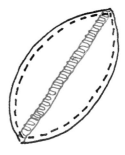

5: Right sides together, machine-stitch the serged leaves to the plain leaves. Use a scant ¼" seam allowance.

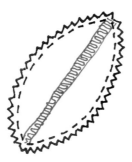

6: Trim the seam allowance with pinking shears to help reduce the bulk.

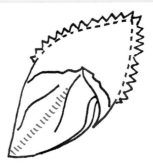

7: Turn the leaves through the slashed fabric. Press leaves and set aside.

QUILT

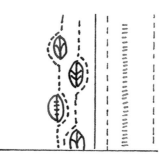

1: Layer quilt top, batting and backing. Baste for quilting.

2: Quilt vertical lines in the large white background rectangle and in the small white rectangles of the left border. Outline quilt along the leaves of the brown print rectangles.

3: Trim the excess batting and backing even with the quilt top.

FINISH

1: Set up the serger for a narrow two-thread overlock stitch using green thread. Refer to *Practicing Stitches—Overlock Stitch* (page 15) for more information.

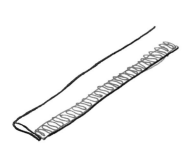

2: With wrong sides together, press the 1" bias stem strips in half lengthwise. Overlock stitch the raw edges trimming slightly.

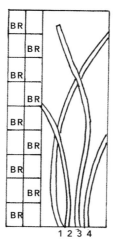

3: Using the quilt photo as an additional placement guide, place 4 stems on the background curving into graceful lines. Curve stems 1 and 4 off the right side of the quilt. Curve stem 2 to the left border. Turn under the raw edge of stem 2 and hand-stitch. Curve stem 3 to the left top. The top leaf will cover the end of stem 3.

4: Quilt the stems to the quilt by stitching along the inside edge of the overlock stitching.

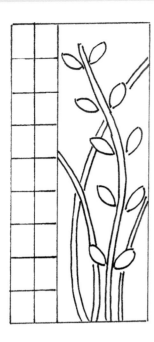

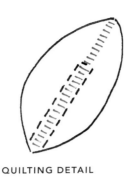

QUILTING DETAIL

5: Place 5 sets of leaves along stem 3. Quilt the leaves to the quilt by stitching ⅔ of the way up the leaf along the ladder stitching. Stitch across the ladder stitching and stitch down on the opposite side of the ladder stitching. This will leave the sides of the leaf loose for a dimensional look.

Reproduce templates at 100%

SIMPLY LEAFY 2 LEAF PATTERN

6: Piece the 2" white binding with a diagonal seam. With wrong sides together, press in half lengthwise. Bind the top, right side and bottom of the quilt with a continuous white binding. Refer to *Quilting Terms & Techniques–Continous Binding* (pages 21–22) for additional information. Fold the binding to the back and hand-stitch.

7: With wrong sides together, press the brown 2" binding strip in half lengthwise. Bind the left side of the quilt with an overlapped binding. Refer to *Quilting Terms & Techniques–Binding with Overlapped Corners* (page 23) for tips on finishing the ends of the binding.

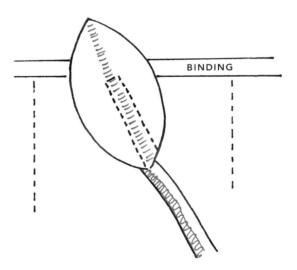

BINDING

8: Attach the final leaf at the tip of stem 3. The top ⅓ of the leaf will extend beyond the top edge of the quilt.

9: Hand-stitch a rod pocket to the back of the quilt. Add a label.

SING THE HARMONIES

Is there anything more exciting than the striking harmony of complementary colors used to their best advantage? Across from each other on the color wheel, red and green keep your eyes vibrating. Complements beget compliments, and you're sure to receive many on this quilt that combines flatlock stitching with appliqué.

Serger skills include: Flatlock stitching using the ladder stitch and the looper stitch, disengaging the cutting blade

Finished size: 31" × 31"

Fabric	Cut	Into	For
Red/green batik	4 strips, 4" × WOF	4 rectangles, 4" × 14"	Borders
		16 rectangles, 1½" × 4"	Borders
		32 rectangles, 1½" × 4"	Flowers
		From the remaining fabric, 32 large leaves*	Leaves
Background	4 blocks, 13" × 13"		Blocks
Red batik	2 strips, 4" × WOF	8 squares, 4" × 4", cut diagonally into 16 half-square triangles	Flowers
		4 squares, 4" × 4"	Border corners
		16 rectangles, 1½" × 4"	Borders
	4 strips, 2" × WOF		Binding
Green solid	3 strips, 2" × WOF	2 small leaves*	Small leaves
		From the remaining fabric, 16 sepals*	Flower sepals

* Attach fusible web prior to cutting.

Serger Setup:

Flatlock Stitch	Left Needle	Right Needle	Upper Looper	Lower Looper	Stitch Length	Stitch Width	Stitch Finger
2-thread wide	1.5	—	Attach 2-thread converter	6	N	N	N
2-thread narrow	—	1.5	Attach 2-thread converter	6	N	N	N

Serger Threading:

Flatlock Stitch	Left Needle	Right Needle	Upper Looper	Lower Looper
Wide (Stems)	Red 50 wt cotton variegated	—	—	Purple/green
Narrow (Leaves)	—	Red 50 wt cotton	—	Purple/green variegated
Narrow (Flowers, border piecing)	—	Purple/green variegated	—	Red 50 wt cotton
Narrow (Attaching borders)	—	Red 50 wt cotton	—	Purple/green variegated

Materials

1 yd. red/green batik (flowers, leaves, borders)

1 yd. neutral background (blocks)

¾ yd. red batik (flowers, borders, binding)

⅜ yd. solid green (flowers, leaves)

Red thread

Purple/green variegated thread

1 yd. batting

1 yd. backing fabric, rod pocket

1¼ yd. paper backed fusible web

12½" square ruler

Seam sealant

Basic serging and quilting tools and supplies

8" × 8" clear vinyl

permanent marker for writing on vinyl

Tip

Choose tightly woven fabrics such as batiks for less fraying and stronger flatlock stitched seams.

CONSTRUCT

STEMS

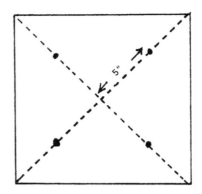

1: Set up your serger for a wide two-thread flatlock stitch. Consult your owner's manual for specific directions for your serger. Refer to *Practicing Stitches—Flatlock Stitch* (page 16) for additional information on this stitch.

2: Thread the serger with purple/green thread in the looper and red thread in the needle. Disengage the cutting blade.

3: With wrong sides together, press the background squares diagonally into 4 quarters. Mark 5" from the center of the square on each diagonal line.

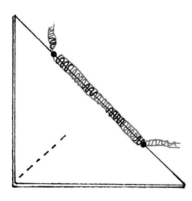

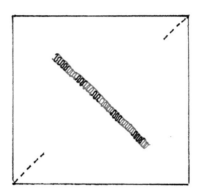

4: Flatlock stitch one diagonal line starting at the 5" mark, stitching across the center and serging off at the second 5" mark. Approximately half of the stitch width will extend beyond the fabric edge. It is helpful to disengage the cutting blade so you don't cut the fabric as you begin serging. The ends of the serging will later be covered by the appliqué.

5: Pull the fabric open to flatten the stitches. You will see the purple/green looper stitch on the right side of the fabric.

6: With wrong sides together, refold on the second diagonal line. Flatlock stitch the second diagonal line. Again, extend the stitch beyond the folded edge and start and finish at the 5" marks.

7: Pull the fabric open to flatten stitches. Press. Trim the serging thread tails. Make 4 blocks.

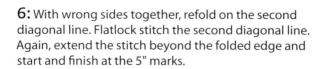

LEAVES

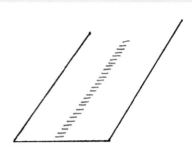

1: Change the needle to the right position for a narrow flatlock stitch.

2: Press the 2" strips lengthwise with right sides together. Stitch a flatlock stitch along the pressed edge. Approximately half of the stitch width will extend beyond the fabric edge.

3: Pull the stitches open to flatten. You will see a red ladder stitch on the right side of the fabric.

WRONG SIDE OF FABRIC

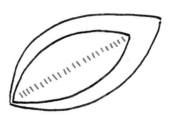

4: Trace the small leaf pattern on the paper side of the fusible web. Make 32. Rough-cut leaving a small margin beyond the traced line. Adhere to the wrong side of the green strips. Center each leaf on the flatlock stitching.

5: Trim the small green leaves on the traced lines. Set aside.

6: Trace the large leaf pattern on the paper side of the fusible web. Make 32. Adhere to the wrong side of the remaining red/green batik fabric.

7: Trim the large red/green leaves on the traced lines. Remove the paper from the back of the small leaves and center at the base of the large leaves. Do not remove the paper from the large leaves. Press the small leaves onto the large leaves.

FLOWERS

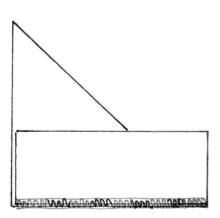

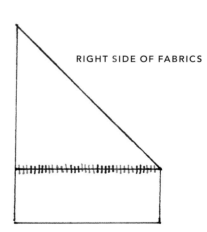

RIGHT SIDE OF FABRICS

1: Rethread the serger with the purple/green variegated thread in the needle and the red thread in the looper. Re-engage the cutting blade, if you have not done so.

2: With right sides together, flatlock stitch a 1½" × 4" rectangle to a 4" side of a half-square triangle. Run the fabric along the edge of the cutter only trimming off threads.

3: Pull the fabrics open to flatten. You will see purple/green ladder stitches on the right side of the fabric. Make 16.

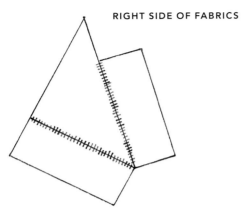

RIGHT SIDE OF FABRICS

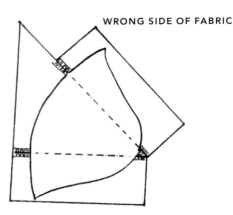

WRONG SIDE OF FABRIC

4: With right sides together, flatlock stitch a 1½" × 4" rectangle to the long side of the half-square triangle as shown. Again, run the fabric along the edge of the cutter only trimming off threads. Pull the fabric open to flatten and press.

5: Trace the flower pattern on the paper side of the fusible web. Rough cut. Place the fusible web on the wrong side of the flower units matching the dashed pattern lines to the pieced seam lines. Press to adhere the fusible web to the back of the flowers. Make 16 flowers.

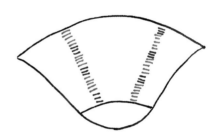

6: Trim the edges of the flowers on the traced lines.

7: Trace the sepal pattern on the fusible web and adhere to the wrong side of the solid green fabric. Trim. Make 16 flower sepals.

8: Remove the paper from the sepals. Do not remove the paper from the back of the flowers. Position the sepal on the flower and press in place.

PIECED BORDER

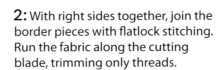

1: Lay out the borders in the following order: 1½" red/green rectangle, 1½" red rectangle, 1½" red/green rectangle, 1½" red rectangle, 14" red/green rectangle, 1½" red rectangle, 1½" red/green rectangle, 1½" red rectangle and 1½" red/green rectangle.

2: With right sides together, join the border pieces with flatlock stitching. Run the fabric along the cutting blade, trimming only threads.

3: Pull the fabric open to reveal the purple/green ladder stitches. Make 4 borders.

ASSEMBLE

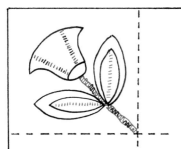

1: Remove the paper from the appliqué pieces and position on the background squares. For easy placement, use a permanent marker to trace the appliqué placement guide onto clear vinyl. Place the vinyl guide over the background and slide the flowers and leaves into position. Remove the placement guide and press the appliqué pieces in place. Repeat for each quarter of the block. Make 4 blocks.

2: Optional machine-stitching: The appliqué on this project is fused in place without stitching. You may choose to machine-stitch around the pieces for additional strength or decorative purposes.

3: Center the appliquéd design and trim the blocks to 12½" × 12½". With right sides together, machine-stitch the blocks together.

4: Rethread the serger with red thread in the right needle and purple/green thread in the lower looper.

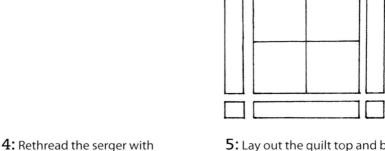

5: Lay out the quilt top and borders.

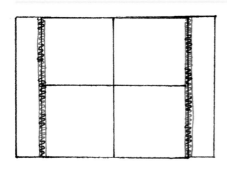

6: With wrong sides together, flatlock stitch the side borders to the quilt. Stitch with the red border on top. Run the fabric along the cutting blade and trim only threads. Pull the fabric open to flatten the stitch. The looper stitch will be showing on the right side of the quilt top.

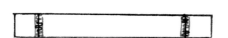

7: With wrong sides together, flatlock stitch the corners to the top and bottom borders. Stitch with the red corner on top. Again, run the fabric along the cutting blade, trimming only threads. Flatten the stitches.

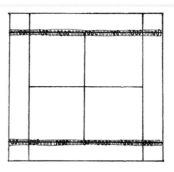

8: With wrong sides together, flatlock stitch the top and bottom borders to the quilt top. Flatten the stitches. Press the completed quilt top.

QUILT AND FINISH

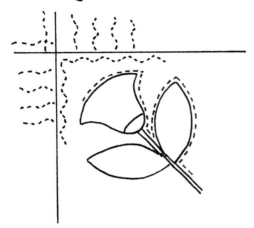

1: Layer the quilt top, batting and backing. Baste for quilting. Outline quilt the appliquéd flowers and leaves. Quilt a wavy line along the border and quilt wavy vertical lines in the border.

2: Diagonally piece the 2" binding strips. Press in half lengthwise. Bind the quilt with a continuous binding. Refer to *Quilting Terms & Techniques—Continuous Binding* (pages 21–22) for further instruction.

3: Add a rod pocket and a label.

Reproduce templates at 100%

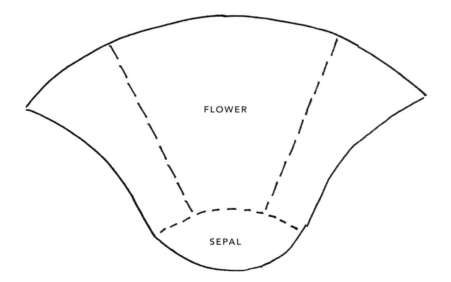

FLOWER

SEPAL

LARGE LEAF

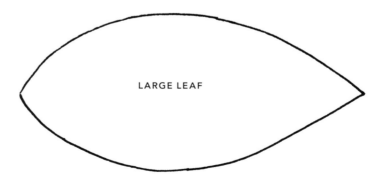

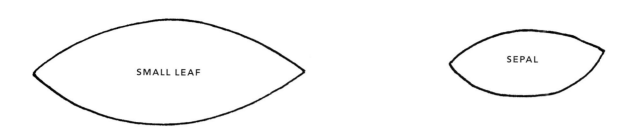

SMALL LEAF

SEPAL

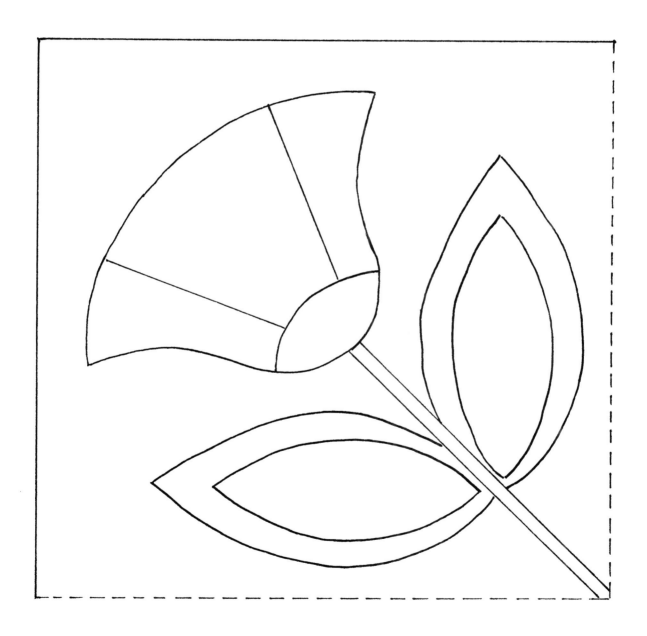

GARDEN ARBOR

Slip into the tranquility of a secret garden surrounded by a colorful floral trellis. Combine large- and small-scale floral prints and set them off with enchanting stripes and a bold lattice border.

Serger skills include: Rolled edge, serging with decorative threads

Finished size: 31" × 38"

Fabric	Cut	Into	For
Light green solid	2 strips, 5½" × WOF	2 rectangles, 5½" × 32¼"	Lattice border
	2 strips, 4" × WOF	2 rectangles, 4" × 22¼"	Top/bottom borders
		5 squares, 1¾" × 1¾"	Sashing
Purple print	4 strips, 2" × WOF		Lattice
	2 strips, 2" × WOF		Binding
	2 strips, 1¾" × WOF	2 rectangles, 1¾" × 14½"	Sashing
		2 rectangles, 1¾" × 9½"	Sashing
	2 strips, 1" × WOF, pressed lengthwise	4 folded strips, ½" × 12½"	Folded trim
		4 folded strips, ½" × 2½"	Folded trim
Turquoise print	4 strips, 2" × WOF		Lattice
	3 strips, 1¾" × WOF	2 rectangles, 1¾" × 29¾"	Sashing
		2 rectangles, 1¾" × 19¾"	Sashing
	1 strip, 1" × WOF, pressed lengthwise	4 folded strips, ½" × 9½"	Folded trim
Large floral print	1 strip, 12½" × WOF	4 rectangles, 7½" × 12½"	Blocks
	1 strip, 4" × WOF	4 rectangles, 4" × 5½"	Border corners
		4 squares, 2½" × 2½"	Blocks
Small floral print	2 strips, 2½" × WOF	4 rectangles, 2½" × 12½"	Blocks
Multicolored stripe	1 strip, 2½" × WOF	4 rectangles, 2½" × 7½"	Blocks
	2 strips, 2" × WOF		Binding

Serger Setup:

	Left Needle	Right Needle	Upper Looper	Lower Looper	Stitch Length	Stitch Width	Stitch Finger
Rolled Edge	—	N	2.5	9	N	N	R

Serger Threading:

Left Needle	Right Needle	Upper Looper	Lower Looper
—	50 wt cotton	No. 8 perle cotton*	50 wt cotton

*Note: If perle cotton is purchased in a ball, it may not feed consistently and may need to be rewound onto an empty spool.

Materials

¾ yd. light green solid (borders, sashing corners)

¾ yd. purple tone-on-tone print (lattice, sashing, folded trim, binding)

⅝ yd. turquoise tone-on-tone print (lattice, sashing, folded trim)

¾ yd. large-scale floral print (blocks, border corners)

⅜ yd. small-scale floral print (blocks)

⅜ yd. multi-colored stripe (blocks, binding)

50 gr. spool dark brown No. 8 perle cotton thread (turquoise lattice rolled edge)

50 gr. spool purple No. 8 perle cotton thread (purple lattice rolled edge)

2 spools dark brown 50 wt cotton thread (serging)

2 spools purple 50 wt cotton thread (serging)

35" × 42" batting

1⅓ yd. backing fabric, rod pocket

Fabric glue stick

Basic serging and quilting tools and supplies

CONSTRUCT

BLOCKS (MAKE 4)

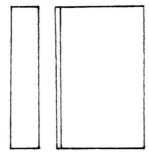

1: Machine-baste the purple folded trim to the left 12½" side of the large floral rectangle.

2: With right sides together, stitch a 2½" small floral rectangle to the large floral rectangle. Catch the basted trim strip in the stitching. Press seams toward the small floral strip.

3: Baste the turquoise folded trim on the lower edge of the block.

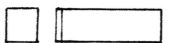

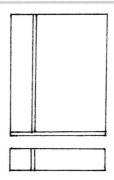

4: Baste the 2½" purple folded trim to the left end of the striped rectangle.

5: Stitch the large floral corner block to the striped rectangle, catching in the folded trim. Press the seams toward the corner.

6: Complete the block by stitching the striped unit to the lower edge of the floral unit. Catch the folded trim in the seam. Press the seams toward the striped unit.

LATTICE BORDERS (MAKE 2)

RIGHT SIDE UP

45°   5½"

1: Set up the serger for a rolled edge. Refer to *Practicing Stitches—Rolled Edge* (page 17) for additional information on this stitch.

2: Serge a rolled edge on both lengthwise edges of the 4 purple lattice strips and the 4 turquoise lattice strips. Place the strips right side up on the serger. Trim the edges slightly so you finish with a 1½" strip. The purple strips will be stitched with the purple perle cotton in the upper looper and the turquoise strips will be stitched with the brown perle cotton in the upper looper.

3: Place a purple strip right side up on the cutting board. Trim a 45-degree angle at the start of the strip. Cut 5½" lattice strips. Cut 16 purple lattice strips. Save the remainder of the rolled edge strips for smaller cuts to fill in the corners of the trellis.

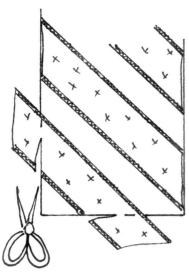

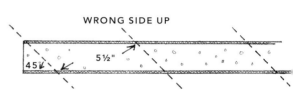

5½"

45°

4: Place the first purple strip on the lower right corner of the light green lattice border. Place the 7 remaining lattice strips 1" apart ending on the upper left corner of the border. Use a glue stick to hold the strips in place.

5: Fill in the corners with lattice strips cut from the remainder of the rolled edge strips. Place strips 1" apart. Make 2 borders.

6: For the turquoise lattice strips, place the rolled edge strip on the cutting board with the wrong side up. Trim a 45-degree angle at the start of the strip. Cut 5½" lattice strips. Cut 16 turquoise lattice strips. Save the remainder of the rolled edge strips for smaller cuts to fill in the corners of the trellis.

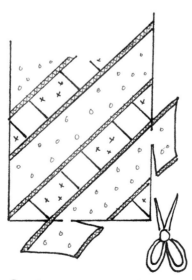

7: Place the first turquoise strip on the lower left corner of the light green lattice border. Place the 7 remaining lattice strips 1" apart ending on the upper right corner of the border. The turquoise strips will cross over the purple lattice strips. Use a fabric glue stick to hold them in place.

8: Fill in the corners with lattice strips cut from the remainder of the rolled edge strips. Place strips 1" apart. Make 2 borders.

ASSEMBLE

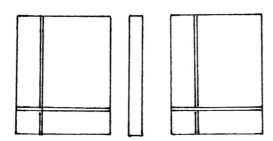

1: With right sides of the fabrics together, stitch a block, a purple sashing strip and a second block together as shown. Make two.

2: Stitch the two remaining purple sashing strips to a light green sashing corner.

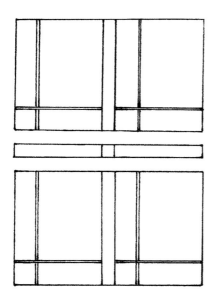

3: Stitch the block rows and the center sashing row together as shown.

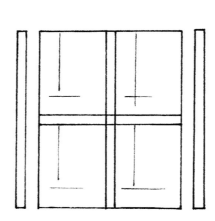

4: Stitch the 29¾" turquoise sashing strips to the sides of the quilt top.

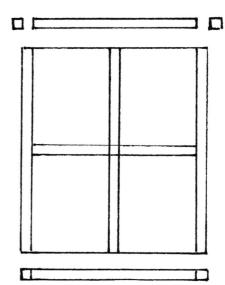

5: Add the light green corner squares to the ends of the 19¾" turquoise sashing strips. Stitch the sashing to the top and bottom of the quilt top.

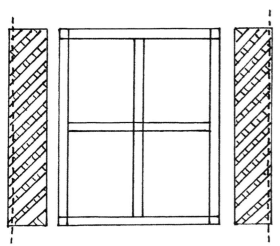

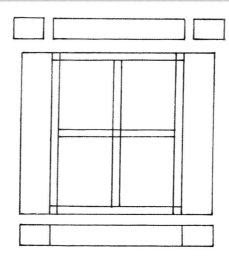

6: Stitch the lattice borders to the sides of the quilt. Staystitch along the outer border edge to keep the strips secure while quilting the wall hanging.

7: Add the corners to the top and bottom borders. Stitch the borders to the quilt completing the quilt top.

QUILT AND FINISH

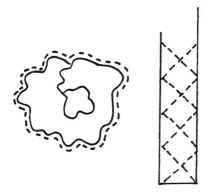

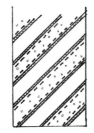

1: Layer the quilt top, batting and backing. Baste for quilting. Outline quilt the floral blocks. Stitch diagonal crosshatching in the sashing.

2: Quilt on the edges of the turquoise lattice strips. (The purple strips are not stitched.) Stitch a feather or other decorative design on the plain green borders.

3: With wrong sides together, press the purple binding strips in half lengthwise. Bind the sides of the quilt with an overlapped binding. Refer to *Quilting Terms & Techniques—Binding with Overlapped Corners* (page 23) for further instruction.

4: With wrong sides together, press the striped binding strips in half lengthwise and bind the top and bottom of the quilt.

5: Add a rod pocket and label to the back of your project.

ARBOR AWNINGS TABLE TOPPER

Enhance the look of your Garden Arbor wall hanging by adding the **Arbor Awnings** *table topper to your decor. Choose a large floral print for the center and enrich its character with wavy striped awnings and lattice corner posts.*

Serger skills include: Rolled edge, serging with decorative threads

Finished size: 40" × 40"

Fabric	Cut	Into	For
Large floral print	1 square, 30½" × 30½"		Center
Multicolored stripe	4 strips, 5½" × WOF	4 rectangles, 5½" × 30½"	Borders
Purple print	2 strips, 2" × WOF		Lattice
	7 bias strips, 2"× 24.5", pieced to 168"		Binding
Turquoise print	2 strips, 2" × WOF		Lattice
	4 strips, 1" × WOF, pressed lengthwise	4 strips, ½" × 30½"	Folded trim
Light green solid	1 strip, 5½" × width of fabric	4 squares, 5½" × 5½"	Corners

Serger Setup:

Overlock Stitch	Left Needle	Right Needle	Upper Looper	Lower Looper	Stitch Length	Stitch Width	Stitch Finger
Rolled edge	—	N	2.5	9	2.5	N	R

Serger Threading:

Left Needle	Right Needle	Upper Looper	Lower Looper
—	50 wt cotton	No. 8 perle cotton	50 wt cotton

Materials

1 yd. large-scale floral print (table topper center)

⅞ yd. multi-colored stripe (border)

¾ yd. purple tone-on-tone print (binding, lattice)

½ yd. turquoise tone-on-tone print (lattice, folded trim)

⅜ yd. light green solid (corner background)

Purple No. 8 perle cotton thread (purple lattice rolled edge)

Dark brown No. 8 perle cotton thread (turquoise lattice rolled edge)

2 spools purple 50 wt cotton thread (serging rolled edge)

2 spools dark brown 50 wt cotton thread (serging rolled edge)

44" × 44" batting

1¼ yd. backing

Fabric glue stick

Basic serging and quilting tools and supplies

CONSTRUCT

1: Set up the serger for a rolled edge. Refer to *Practicing Stitches—Rolled Edge* (page 17) for additional information on this stitch.

2: Serge a rolled edge on both lengthwise edges of the 2" purple lattice strips and the 2" turquoise lattice strips. Place the strips right side up on the serger. Trim the edges slightly so you finish with a 1½" strip. The purple strips will be stitched with the purple perle cotton in the upper looper and the turquoise will be stitched with the brown perle cotton in the upper looper.

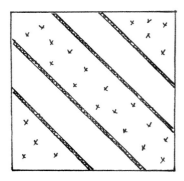

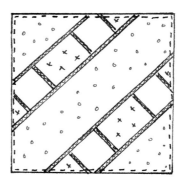

3: Place a purple lattice strip diagonally across the light green corner square. Center the lattice on the square and trim to fit. Secure with a fabric glue stick. Place additional strips 1" from the center strip. Glue in place.

4: Place a turquoise lattice strip diagonally across the opposite corners. Center the lattice on the square and trim to fit. Secure with a fabric glue stick. Place additional strips 1" from the center strip. Glue in place. Machine-baste to secure ends of lattice. Make 4 blocks with the turquoise and purple lattice strips.

ASSEMBLE

1: Machine-baste the turquoise folded trim to all edges of the floral center square.

2: With right sides together, serge or stitch the borders to the sides of the center, catching the basted trim in the seam.

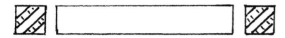 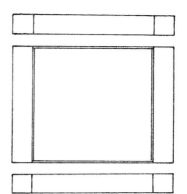

3: With right sides together, serge or stitch the lattice corners to the top and bottom borders.

4: Add the top and bottom borders to the quilt, catching the basted trim in the seam.

QUILT AND FINISH

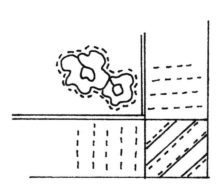
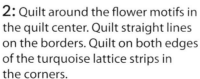

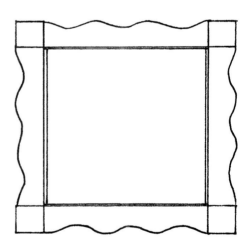

1: Layer the quilt top, batting and backing. Baste for quilting.

2: Quilt around the flower motifs in the quilt center. Quilt straight lines on the borders. Quilt on both edges of the turquoise lattice strips in the corners.

3: Use the awning template (page 92) to trim the curved edges of the striped borders. Follow the diagrammed steps for making a full-size paper template. Center the template on the outer edge of the quilt border and trim.

4: Press the bias binding in half lengthwise. Bind the quilt with a continuous binding. Refer to *Quilting Terms & Techniques—Continuous Binding* (pages 21–22) for further instruction.

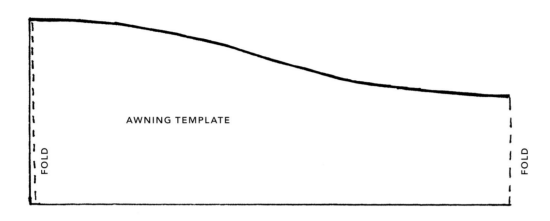

AWNING TEMPLATE

FOLD

FOLD

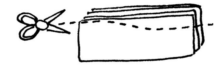

ACCORDION FOLD 30" PAPER STRIP

TRIM TO SHAPE

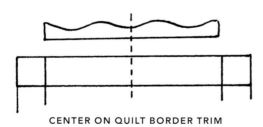

CENTER ON QUILT BORDER TRIM

BERRIES & BLOOMS

Combine a little R & R with your B & B. Of course, we are speaking of a double-ruched delight made of a luscious berries and blooms fabric. Elegant trimmings and breathtaking fabric highlight this dramatically simple quilt.

Serger skills include: Rolled edge, overlock stitch, serging with decorative threads

Finished size: 22" × 28"

Fabric	Cut	For
Floral print	1 rectangle, 16½" × 16½" 2 rectangles, 2½" × 16½"	Center block Side blocks
Dark purple print	4 strips, 2" × WOF 2 strips, 2½" × WOF	Ruched bands Pieced borders
Light green/lilac stripe	2 strips, 2½" × WOF 3 strips, 1½" × WOF	Pieced borders Ruched trim, flowers
Light green batik	4 strips, 1" wide × 16½" 3 strips, 2" × WOF 2 strips, 1½" × WOF	Side borders Binding Ruched flowers
Muslin	4 strips, 4" wide × 16½"	Underlining for ruched bands

Serger Setup:

	Left Needle	Right Needle	Upper Looper	Lower Looper	Stitch Length	Stitch Width	Stitch Finger
4-thread overlock (gathering)	8	8	N	N	4.5	N	N
Rolled edge	—	N	2.5	9	N	N	R

Serger Threading:

	Left Needle	Right Needle	Upper Looper	Lower Looper
4-thread overlock (gathering)	50 wt cotton	50 wt cotton	50 wt cotton	50 wt cotton
Rolled edge	—	50 wt cotton	No. 8 perle cotton	50 wt cotton

Materials

⅝ yd. large-scale floral print (center block)

⅝ yd. dark purple tone-on-tone print (ruched bands, pieced borders)

½ yd. light green/lilac stripe (ruched trim, pieced borders)

½ yd. light green batik (side borders, ruched flowers, binding)

4 spools purple cotton thread

Pearl iridescent thread (quilting)

¼ yd. muslin (underlining)

26" × 32" batting

1 yd. backing, rod pocket

Basic serging and quilting tools and supplies

No. 8 purple perle cotton thread

CONSTRUCT

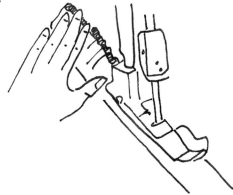
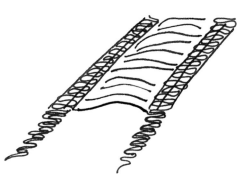

1: Set up the serger for a four-thread overlock stitch. Refer to *Practicing Stitches–Overlock Stitch* (page 14) for additional information on gathering fabric with your serger.

2: To make the ruched (or gathered) bands, overlock stitch on the right side of one 2" dark purple strip. Trim the raw edge slightly as you stitch. Serge 1" and then gently hold the strip against the back of the serger foot to increase the density of the gathers on the strip. Leave long tails at the start and finish of your serging.

3: Serge the second long side of the strip to gather it. You will not have to hold the strip behind the foot because the first gathered side holds the gathers for the second side. Serge slowly to keep the edge straight as you serge and to avoid stitching in pleats. Again, leave long tails at the start and finish of your serging.

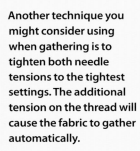
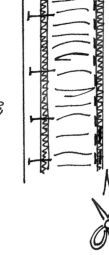
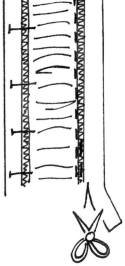
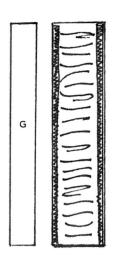

4: Pull the right needle thread to adjust the gathers but be careful not to pull out your thread. Gather to 16½". Make 4.

5: To stabilize your ruched bands, pin them onto the muslin underlining strips. Machine-baste and trim the underlining to the width of the gathered strip.

6: With right sides together, machine-stitch 1½" light green strips (G) to the ruched bands. Increase your ¼" seam allowance slightly to cover the gathering stitches.

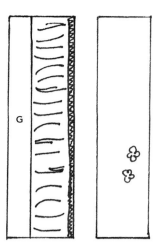

7: With right sides together, stitch a 2½" floral strip to a ruched strip as shown. Again, increase the width of your seam allowance slightly to cover the gathering stitches. Press seam allowances away from the ruched strip. Make 2.

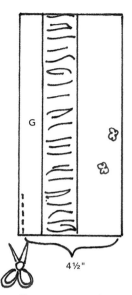

4½"

8: Trim these units to measure 4½" by trimming off the light green strips (G), as needed.

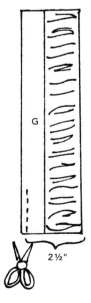

2½"

9: Trim the 2 remaining ruched units to measure 2½" by trimming off the light green strip (G).

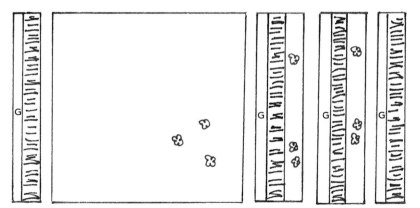

10: Stitch the ruched units to the large floral center block as indicated in the diagram.

ASSEMBLE

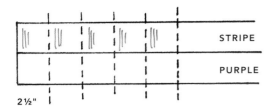

STRIPE

PURPLE

2½"

1: With right sides together, serge or machine stitch the 2½" light green/lilac strips to the dark purple strips. Crosscut into 2½" units. Cut 21 units.

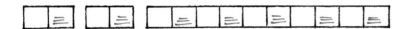

2: With right sides together, join 7 units together for the top border, rotating the units in order to alternate the fabrics. Make 3.

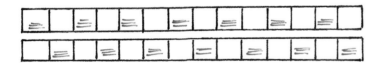

3: With right sides together, join two rows of 7 units together. Stitch the rows together for the bottom border.

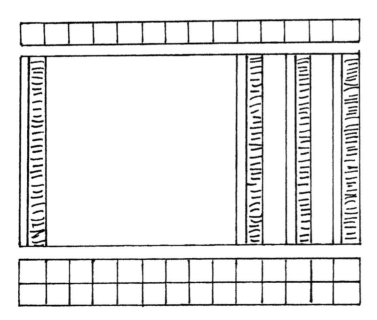

4: Stitch the top and bottom borders to the quilt.

QUILT AND FINISH

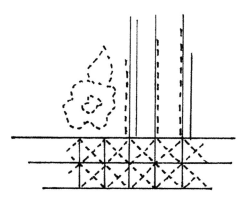  

1: Layer the quilt top, batting and backing. Baste for quilting. Echo quilt the floral center. Stitch in the ditch along the ruched bands and crosshatch the borders.

2: Stitch the binding strips together with diagonal seams. With wrong sides together, press in half lengthwise. Bind the quilt with a continuous binding. Refer to *Quilting Terms & Techniques—Continuous Binding* (pages 21–22) for further instruction.

3: Set up your serger for a rolled edge. Refer to *Practicing Stitches—Rolled Edge* (page 17) for additional information on this stitch.

4: With the right side of the fabric facing up, serge a rolled edge on both long edges of the 1½" light green/lilac stripe ruched trim/flower strips. Serge a rolled edge on both edges of the 1½" light green ruched flower strips. Trim the fabric slightly as you serge so the completed strip is 1".

5: For the ruched trim, cut 3 strips, 18" long from the light green/lilac stripe rolled edge strips.

6: Mark one edge of the fabric strip. The marks will be 1" apart. Start marking ½" from the right end of the strip. Mark the second edge of the fabric strip. Start marking 1" from the right end. Mark 1" apart. The marks should be centered midway between the marks on the first side.

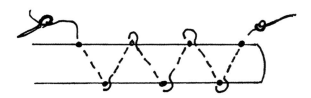 

7: Thread a large needle with perle cotton and knot one end. Starting on the back side of the strip, stitch from right to left. Stitch diagonally across the strip from the first mark to the bottom mark. End with the thread on the right side of the strip. Wrap the thread around to the back of the strip and continue stitching. Stitch to the top mark. Again, wrap the thread to the back of the strip and stitch to the bottom mark. Continue across the strip.

8: Pull the thread to gather the ruching. Gather the ruching as you go along. When you have completed the entire strip, gather the ruching to 9" and tie off the ruching thread. Make 2. These will be used on the bottom border.

9: Repeat these steps for the shorter 6" top border trim. Ruche until you a 7" length and tie off your ruching thread. Trim off the excess strip.

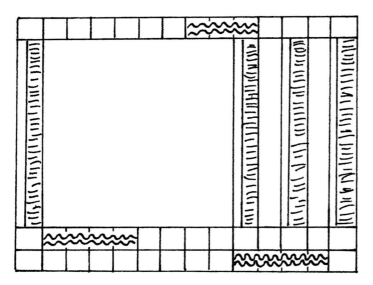

10: Turn under the raw ends of the ruched strips. Hand-stitch in place on the quilt.

11: For the large ruched flowers, cut 2 strips, 20" long from the light green/lilac striped strips and 2 strips, 20" long from the light green batik. For the small flowers, cut 2 strips, 10" long from the light green batik.

12: Ruche the strips as you did for the trim. Use the entire strip. Tie off the ruching thread and join the ends to form a circular flower shape.

13: Hand-stitch the flowers to the quilt. Refer to the quilt photo for color placement.

14: To complete the quilt, add a rod pocket and a label.

DOWN THE PATHWAY

Along the path, we see a bunny buffet of floral delight and tasty offerings ready for nibbling. Have fun displaying your serging talents as you construct a tulip garden with dimensional flowers and leaves. This art quilt features a nontraditional construction method for ease in quilting. Because you will be pressing and fusing over your threads and batting, it is very important to pretest your choices.

Serger skills include: Flatlock stitch, overlock stitch, rolled edge

Finished size: 17" × 36"

Fabric	Cut	For
Pale yellow	1 rectangle, 14½" × 34½"	Background
Medium/dark green	1 strip, 2" × WOF 6 rectangles, 3" × 6" 9 fused leaves using leaf pattern A* 12 fused ¼" wide × 9" bias cut stems*	Binding Leaves Leaves Stems
Medium/light green	1 rectangle, 2½" × 38" 2 rectangles, 2½" × 14" 2 strips, 2" × WOF	Top border Side borders Binding
Rose batik	2 strips, 2½" × WOF	Tulips
Multicolored stripe	1 rectangle, 3½" × 36½"	Bottom border

* Attach fusible web prior to cutting.

Serger Setup:

	Left Needle	Right Needle	Upper Looper	Lower Looper	Stitch Length	Stitch Width	Stitch Finger
Flatlock - Narrow (Background)	—	1.5	Insert 2-thread converter	4.5	N	N	N
Overlock - Narrow (Leaves)	—	N	N	N	2	N	N
Rolled edge	—	N	N	9	1	N	R

Serger Threading:

	Left Needle	Right Needle	Upper Looper	Lower Looper
Flatlock - Narrow (Background)	—	Purple/green variegated polyester	—	Medium/light green polyester
Overlock - Narrow (Leaves)	—	Medium/light green polyester	Purple/green variegated polyester	Medium/light green polyester
Rolled edge	—	Purple cotton	Rose/purple variegated	Purple cotton

Materials

½ yd. solid pale yellow (background)

⅝ yd. medium/dark green (stems, leaves, binding)

½ yd. medium/light green (borders, binding)

⅓ yd. rose batik (tulips)

⅛ yd. green/purple multi-colored stripe (bottom border)

Variegated green/purple polyester thread (background, leaves)

2 spools medium/light green polyester thread (background, leaves)

Variegated rose/purple cotton thread (tulips)

2 spools purple cotton thread

Invisible thread (quilting)

24" × 40" cotton batting

1 yd. backing, rod pocket

⅔ yd. paper-backed fusible web or 3 sheets of 9" × 12"

Seam sealant such as Fray Check

Small craft iron

Basic serging and quilting tools and supplies

CONSTRUCT

BACKGROUND

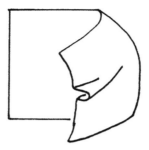 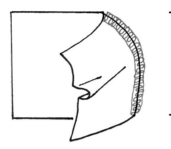

1: Set up the serger for a two-thread flatlock stitch using the green/purple variegated thread in the needle and medium/light green thread in the looper. Refer to *Practicing Stitches—Flatlock Stitch* (page 16) for more information on this stitch.

2: With wrong sides together, lightly press a diagonal, slightly curving line on the background.

3: Disengage your serger's cutting blade. Flatlock stitch along this line, guiding your fabric so half of the stitch extends off the fabric. Pull the fabric to open the stitches. The looper stitch will be showing on the right side of the fabric.

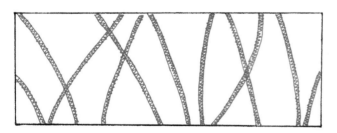 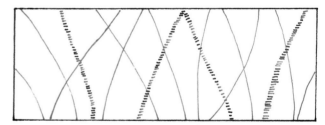

4: Press 10 additional lines and flatlock stitch. Vary the spacing and the curve of the flatlock rows. It is more interesting to have rows curving in both directions. Pull to open stitches before crossing any rows.

5: With right sides together, lightly press 4 diagonal curving lines. Flatlock stitch, extending the stitching off the fabric. Pull to open stitches. The ladder stitch will be showing on the right side of the fabric.

6: Press the background and trim to 12½" × 32½".

NOTES FROM **NANCY**

For those of you who have a chain or cover stitch option with your serger, consider substituting either of these two stitches for the flatlock seam. Follow your owner's manual to set up the stitch and attach the appropriate sewing plate, which covers the blade mechanism. This project is ideal for experimenting with this stitch that is often overlooked by serger owners.

LEAVES AND STEMS

FOLD

MAKE 4   MAKE 2

1: Set up the serger for a narrow overlock stitch using the purple/green variegated thread in the upper looper. You can find further information on this stitch in *Practicing Stitches—Overlock Stitch* (page 15).

2: With wrong sides together, press the 3" × 6" rectangles in half lengthwise. Trim to shape using leaf pattern B.

3: Overlock stitch the curved raw edges of the leaf. Use a seam sealant to secure the threads at the tip of the leaf. Trim threads. Make 4 with the variegated overlock stitching on the right side of the leaf and 2 with the variegated overlock stitching on the left side of the leaf.

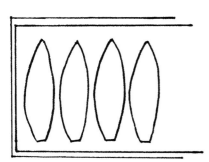

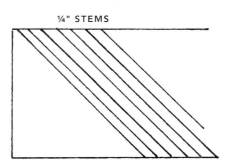

¼" STEMS

4: Trace Leaf A on the paper side of the fusible web. Make 9. Press the fusible web to the wrong side of the medium/dark green fabric. Trim.

5: Press additional fusible web to the wrong side of the medium/dark green fabric to cut 12 bias stems, ¼" × 8"–9". (Shorter lengths may be used by tucking them behind the leaves when fusing to the background.)

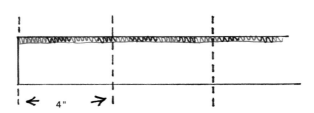

1: Set up the serger for a rolled edge with the variegated thread in the upper looper.

2: With the right side of the fabric up, stitch a rolled edge on one long edge of the 2½" rose strip. Trim the fabric slightly.

3: Crosscut the strip into 4" rectangles.

4: Fold the rectangle into a tube. Drop one edge of the rectangle and stitch a rolled edge, seaming the raw edges. Use a seam sealant to secure the thread ends and trim. Make 12 tulip tubes.

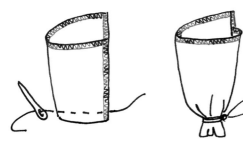
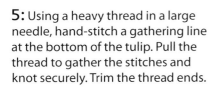

5: Using a heavy thread in a large needle, hand-stitch a gathering line at the bottom of the tulip. Pull the thread to gather the stitches and knot securely. Trim the thread ends.

6: Turn the tulip so the knot is buried inside of the tulip. The vertical rolled edge will be inside the tulip. Make 5.

7: For the remaining 7 tulips, turn first so the vertical rolled edge is inside of the tulip tube. Gather and knot the bottom of the tulip. Turn the tulip back to the right side. The vertical rolled edge will be showing on the outside of the tulip.

ASSEMBLE AND QUILT

MITERING BORDERS

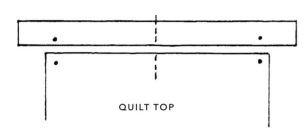

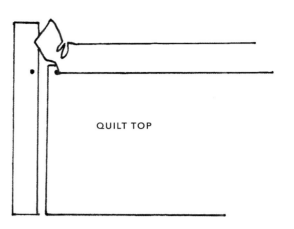

QUILT TOP

QUILT TOP

1: With right sides together, center the top border strip on the quilt top. Machine-stitch the top border to the quilt top. Start and stop the seam at a dot ¼" from the side edges of the quilt top. Secure the stitching at the start and end of the seam.

2: With right sides together and the lower edges even, stitch the side borders to the quilt. Stop stitching ¼" from the top edge and secure the stitching.

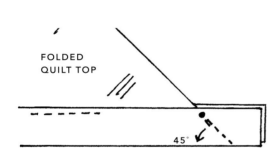

FOLDED QUILT TOP

45°

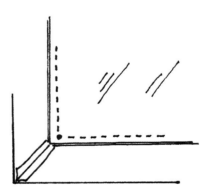

3: Fold the quilt top on a diagonal, aligning the border strips. Mark a 45-degree line from the dot to the edge of the border strip. Pin and stitch the miter. You may stitch from the dot to the border edge or from the edge to the dot, but secure the stitching at the dot.

4: Check the mitered corner before trimming the seam allowance. Press the seam open.

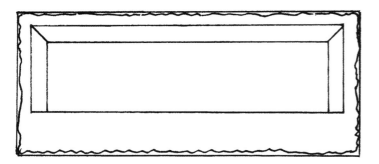

1: Layer the quilt top, batting and backing. Place the quilt top near the top of the sandwich, leaving about 6" of batting and backing at the bottom. Baste for quilting.

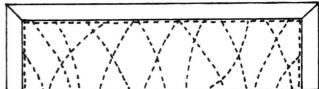

2: Stitch in the ditch between the quilt and the top and side borders. Using invisible thread, quilt along the flatlock stitching lines in the background. Quilt additional lines in the background.

ADDING LEAVES AND STEMS

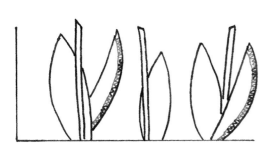

1: Arrange the leaves and stems on the background. Vary the placement of the folded leaves, placing some on top and some behind the fused leaves. Curve the bias stems slightly for more graceful lines.

2: When you are pleased with the arrangement, cover with a press cloth and fuse the leaves and stems in place.

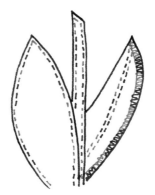

3: Using the purple/green variegated thread, quilt the edges of the fused stems and leaves. Secure the folded leaves to the quilt by quilting up and down the center of the leaf. The loose edges of the folded leaf will give a dimensional look.

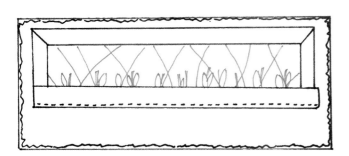

4: With right sides together, machine-stitch the bottom border to the quilt. You will be stitching through the quilt top, the batting and the backing.

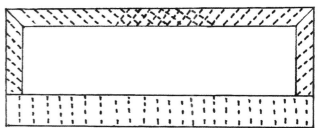

5: Press the bottom border down covering the excess batting and backing at the bottom of the quilt. Using the invisible thread, quilt the borders of the quilt. Quilt diagonal lines in the top and side borders. Quilt vertical lines in the bottom border.

FINISH

1: Fuse the tulips to the tops of the stems. Use a small amount of fusible web behind the tulip and press inside the tube to fuse the tulip to the background. A small craft iron works well for this step. (The tulips may also be hand-stitched in place.)

2: Diagonally piece the medium/ light green border strips. Press in half lengthwise. Bind to the sides and top of the quilt. Refer to *Quilting Terms & Techniques— Continuous Binding* (page 21–22) for further instruction.

3: Press the medium/dark green strip in half lengthwise. Bind the bottom of the quilt with an overlapped binding. Refer back to *Quilting Terms & Techniques–Binding with Overlapped Corners*, steps 4–6 (page 23) for tips on finishing the ends.

4: Add a rod pocket and a label.

Reproduce templates at 100%

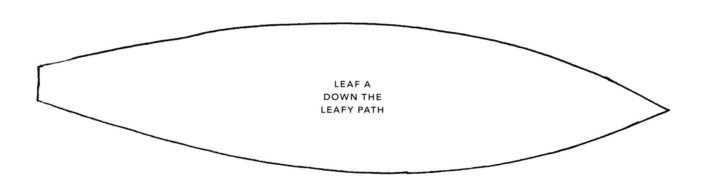

LEAF A
DOWN THE
LEAFY PATH

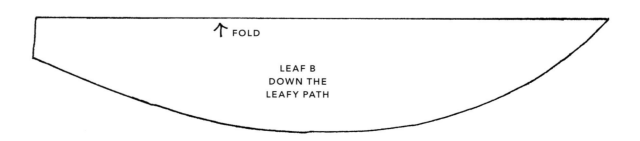

↑ FOLD

LEAF B
DOWN THE
LEAFY PATH

"LOOK AT ME" BAG

There is nothing shy and retiring about this sassy little handbag. Its bright colors and stylish design shout "look at me." Try your serger skills on a quilted project that travels with you rather than adorns your home.

Serger skills include: Flatlock stitch, overlock stitch, gathering

Finished Size: 8" × 12"

Fabric	Cut	For
Multicolored stripe	1 rectangle 18" × 20" 1 strip, 3½" × 30" 2 rectangles, 3½" × 12"	Lining Ruffle Top bands
Multicolored print	1 square 18" × 20" 1 strip, 2" × 12"	Body Handle tabs
Turquoise	2 strips, 1" × WOF	Accent stripes

Serger Setup

	Left Needle	Right Needle	Upper Looper	Lower Looper	Stitch Length	Stitch Width	Stitch Finger
3-thread flatlock (Wide)	—	2	5	6	2	N	N
4-thread overlock (gathering)	8	8	N	N	4.5	N	N
4-thread overlock (seams)	N	N	N	N	N	N	N

Serger Threading:

	Left Needle	Right Needle	Upper Looper	Lower Looper
3-thread flatlock (Wide)	—	Turquoise 30 wt rayon	Turquoise 50 wt cotton	Turquoise 50 wt cotton
4-thread overlock (gathering)	All-purpose polyester serging thread	All-purpose polyester serging thread	All-purpose polyester serging thread	All-purpose polyester serging thread
4-thread overlock (seams)	All-purpose polyester serging thread	All-purpose polyester serging thread	All-purpose polyester serging thread	All-purpose polyester serging thread

Materials

⅞ yd. multi-colored stripe (lining, ruffle, top bands)

⅝ yd. multi-colored print (body, handle tabs)

⅛ yd. solid turquoise (accent stripes)

Turquoise rayon thread (flatlock stitching, quilting, topstitching)

2 spools turquoise cotton thread

4 spools all-purpose polyester serging thread

18" × 18" batting

6" × 12" ultra-firm interfacing

2" × 12" fusible interfacing

6" wide purchased purse handles

Magnetic purse snap

Basic serging and quilting tools and supplies

CONSTRUCT AND QUILT

BODY

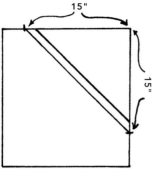

1: On the right side of the body, draw a diagonal line from a dot 15" from the right top corner to a dot 15" down the right side. Cut on the line. Cut a second line 1¼" toward the corner.

2: Set up the serger for a wide three-thread flatlock stitch by removing the right needle. Refer to *Practicing Stitches–Flatlock Stitch* (page 16) for more information on this stitch.

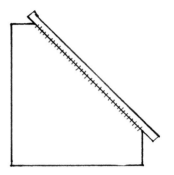

3: With right sides together, flatlock stitch a turquoise accent strip to the diagonal slashed edge of the bag body. Pull the fabrics to open the stitching. You will see a ladder stitch on the right sides of the fabrics.

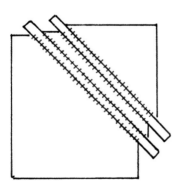

4: With right sides together, center and flatlock stitch the slashed body strip to the turquoise strip. Pull the fabrics to open the stitching. Continue serging the second accent strip and the corner triangle to the body.

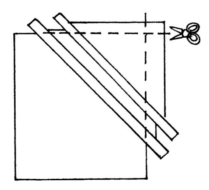

5: Trim the edges even with the main part of the bag body.

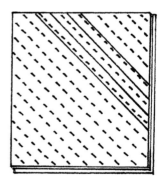

6: Layer the bag body, batting and lining. Baste for quilting. Quilt diagonal lines 1" apart in the same direction as the diagonal accent stripes.

RUFFLE

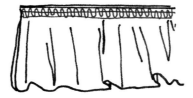

1: Set up the serger for a four-thread overlock stitch. Change threads and replace the right needle. Set up the tensions for gathering.

2: With wrong sides together, press the multicolored ruffle strip in half lengthwise. Overlock stitch gathers along the raw edges of the strip.

3: Set up the serger for a normal overlock stitch by changing from the gathering tension settings to the normal settings.

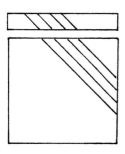

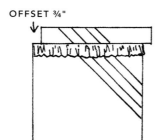

OFFSET ¾"

4: To insert the ruffle into the bag body, cut a 2¼" strip off the top of the bag body, as shown.

5: With right sides together pin the ruffle and the top body strip to the bag body. To keep the accent strips aligned after serging, offset the 2¼" body strip ¾" as shown. Overlock stitch the seam, removing pins as you go.

6: Trim the body to 15" wide × 18" long.

TOP BANDS

1: Fold the top bands in half lengthwise. With right sides together, overlock stitch the ends of the multicolored stripe bands to make 2 bands, 1¾" × 11½". Turn to the right side and press.

2: Insert a 1⅜" × 11⅜" rectangle of ultra-firm interfacing in each of the bands. Following manufacturer's instructions, attach a magnetic purse snap to the inside of the bands. Attach through the interfacing layer for extra strength. Center the snap on the width of the bands. Place the snap closer to the top folded edge of the bands so it does not interfere with serging the bands to the body.

3: Insert a second 1⅜" × 11⅜" interfacing rectangle in each band. This will protect the front of the bands from showing through and wearing from the back of the magnetic snaps. Baste the bottom raw edge of the bands together.

HANDLE TABS

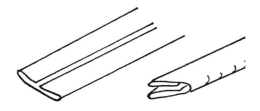 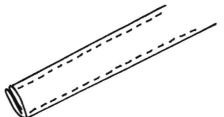 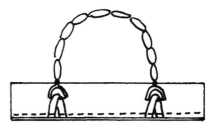

1: To strengthen the handle tabs, fuse interfacing to the wrong side of the 2" × 12" multicolored print strip. Fold the sides to the center of the strip. Press. Fold again so the raw edges are hidden and press.

2: Topstitch along both edges of the ½" × 12" folded strip.

3: Cut into 4 tabs, ½" × 3". Attach the handle to the bag by folding the tabs around the purse handles and basting to the bottom of the bands. Center the handle on the band.

NOTES FROM **NANCY**

When serging a seam that will get above average use, I reinforce the beginning and ending of the seam with a traditional straight stitch. The side seam of this bag would be an ideal place to use your serger and sewing machine in tandem.

ASSEMBLE

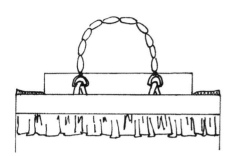

1: With right sides together, center the top bands on the body of the bag. Pin in place. Overlock stitch the bands to the bag, finishing all the raw edges of the top of the bag and removing pins as you serge.

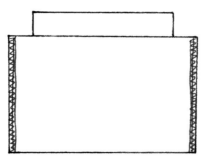

2: With right sides together, fold the bag in half and align the side seams. Overlock stitch the side seams.

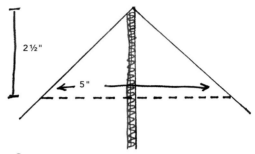

3: To shape the bottom corners of the bag, fold to form a triangle with the side seam centered on the bottom of the bag. Draw a line 2½" down and 5" across. Stitch on the line. For reinforcement, stitch a second seam ⅛" from the first. Repeat for the second bottom corner.

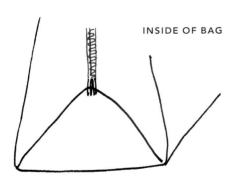

4: To hold the bag shape, fold the corner triangle up and hand-stitch to the side seam.

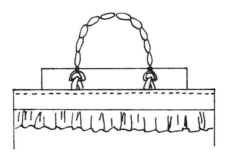

5: To finish the top edges of the bag, press the seam allowances toward the body. Topstitch around the entire bag catching in the seam allowances and forming a neat hem at the top of the side seams.

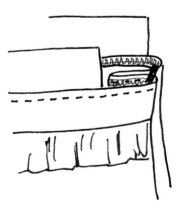

6: With right sides together, stitch a 1" pleat at the top of the side seams to finish the bag.

AND OUT THEY CAME, PANDORA

Are you ready to finish with a flair and test your serging skills making a unique art quilt? And Out They Came, Pandora combines a little of everything in one creative project. Use your flatlock skills to stitch a decorative fat quarter background. Employ overlock stitching to join squares into bold pieced segments. Finish with rolled edges on butterflies that flutter off the surface.

Serger skills include: Flatlock stitching, overlock stitching, rolled edge

Finished size: 23" × 25"

Fabric	Cut	For
Mottled purple	1 rectangle, 18" × 20"	Background
Yellow geometric print	6 strips, 2½" × 20"	Pieced segments
Yellow floral print	6 strips, 2½" × 20"	Pieced segments
Yellow/purple batik	1 circle, 6½" 1 square, 5½" × 5½" 2 squares, 5" × 5" 5 squares, 3" × 3" 4 squares, 2" × 2" 1 square, 1½" × 1½"	Circle Butterfly Butterflies Butterflies Butterflies Butterfly
Yellow tone-on-tone	1 circle, 7½" × 7½"	Circle
Purple print	1 rectangle, 9" × 19"	Lower border

Serger Setup:

	Left Needle	Right Needle	Upper Looper	Lower Looper	Stitch Length	Stitch Width	Stitch Finger
3-thread wide flatlock	—	1	N	7	N	N	N
3-thread wide overlock	—	N	N	N	N	N	N
Rolled edge	—	N	N	7	1.5	N	R

Serger Threading:

	Left Needle	Right Needle	Upper Looper	Lower Looper
3-thread flatlock	—	Red all-purpose polyester serging thread	Purple/red variegated 30 wt cotton	Red all-purpose polyester serging thread
3-thread overlock (background)	—	Red all-purpose polyester serging thread	Purple/red variegated 30 wt cotton	Red all-purpose polyester serging thread
3-thread overlock (pieced segments)	—	Gold 50 wt cotton	Gold 50 wt cotton	Variegated bright colored 40 wt cotton
Rolled edge	—	Gold 50 wt cotton	Gold 40 wt polyester	Gold 50 wt cotton

Materials

Fat quarter mottled purple (background)

Fat quarter yellow geometric print (pieced segments)

Fat quarter yellow floral print (pieced segments)

Fat quarter yellow/purple batik (circle, butterflies)

8" × 8" yellow tone-on-tone (circle)

Fat quarter purple print (lower border)

Variegated purple/red cotton thread

2 spools red all-purpose polyester thread

Variegated bright colored cotton thread

Gold 40 wt polyester specialty thread

2 spools gold 50 wt cotton thread

Invisible thread (top stitching, quilting)

30" × 36" batting

1¼ yd. backing, binding, rod pocket

Seam sealant such as Fray Check

Gold jewelry wire

Small jewelry pliers

Basic serging and quilting tools and supplies

8" × 20" rinse away stabilizer

CONSTRUCT

BACKGROUND

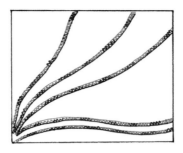

1: Set up the serger for a wide three-thread flatlock stitch. Refer to *Practicing Stitches–Flatlock Stitch* (page 16) for more information on this stitch.

2: With wrong sides together, flatlock stitch 5 lines starting from the lower left corner of the purple fat quarter. Finish the lines at the top right and right side of the fat quarter in a pattern evoking sun rays. Curve the fabric as you stitch for more drama. Pull the fabric to flatten the stitches and press.

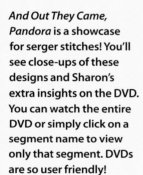
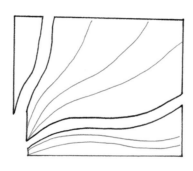

3: Divide the fat quarter into thirds by making two curving cuts in the same direction as the rays.

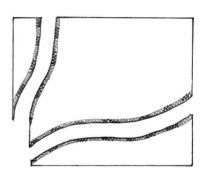

4: Set up the serger for a wide three-thread overlock stitch using the same threads as you used for the flatlock. Overlock stitch the edges of the curved cuts.

PIECED SEGMENTS

1: Change thread colors for the pieced segments.

WRONG SIDES TOGETHER

2: With wrong sides together, overlock stitch a 2½" yellow geometric strip to a yellow floral strip. Press the seam allowances toward the yellow geometric strip. The seam allowances will be exposed on the right side of the fabrics. Make three.

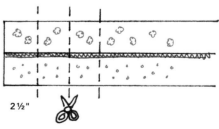

2½"

3: Crosscut into 2½" units. Make 18.

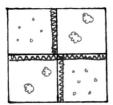

4: With wrong sides together, overlock stitch two units into a four patch, rotating the units so the like fabrics are kitty-corner to each other. Make 9 four patches with the seams exposed on the right sides of the fabrics.

5: With right sides together, serge or machine-stitch a 2½" yellow geometric strip to a yellow floral strip. Press the seam allowances toward the yellow geometric strip. Make three.

6: Crosscut into 2½" units. Make 18.

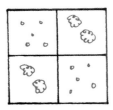

7: With right sides together, overlock stitch two units into a four patch. Rotate the units so the like fabrics are kitty-corner to each other. Make 9 four patches with the seams hidden.

SEGMENT 1

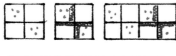

SEGMENT 2

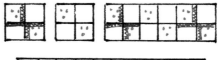

8: Lay out the four patches into rows as shown. Alternate the four patches with the exposed seams with the other 4 patches. With right sides together, serge or machine-stitch the rows. Make 2 of each segment.

SEGMENT 1

SEGMENT 2

9: With right sides together, join the rows of Segment 1, which will be used as the vertical segment. Join the rows of Segment 2, which will be used as the horizontal segment.

BUTTERFLIES

1: Set up the serger for a three-thread rolled edge. Refer to *Practicing Stitches–Rolled Edge* (page 17) for more information.

2: With right sides of the fabric up under the serger, serge a rolled edge on each side of the butterfly squares. Stitch off the edge, trim the threads and secure with a seam sealant. Repeat for all butterfly squares.

3: Shape the butterfly by wrapping gold jewelry wire around the center of the square, forming two wings. With small pliers, curl the ends of the wire to form antennae. Repeat for all the butterflies.

CIRCLES

1: Place a corresponding sized circle of rinse-away stabilizer behind each circle.

2: Serge a rolled edge around the circle. Overlap the serging slightly at the finish, trim the threads and secure with a seam sealant. Repeat for the other circle.

LOWER BORDER

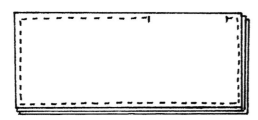 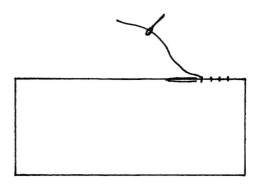

1: Cut a 9" × 19" rectangle of batting and backing. Layer the border and backing, right sides together, on the batting. Stitch around the border leaving an 8" opening for turning on the top near the upper right corner.

2: Turn to the right side and press. Close the opening by fusing or hand-stitching.

ASSEMBLE

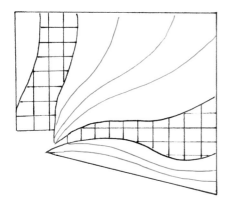

1: Lay the pieced segments under the curved cuts in the background. Spread the background fabric sections to reveal the pieced segments, leaving a slight overlap for seaming. Keep the patches parallel to the quilt edges. Pin in place.

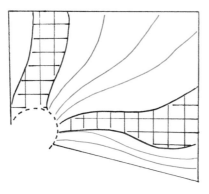

2: Lay the large circle in place, making sure all raw edges will be covered. On the outside edge of the quilt top, the circle should be placed ¼" inside the edge. Draw a chalk line where the circle is placed and remove the circle.

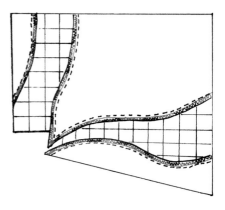

3: Seam the sections together by topstitching with invisible thread. Stitch along the inside edge of the serging stitches.

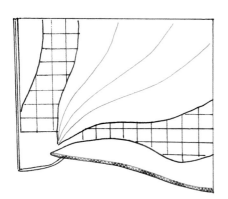

4: Layer the quilt top, batting and backing. Baste for quilting. Cut a curving line on the lower edge of the quilt. Using the red/purple variegated thread, overlock stitch the lower edge. You will be serging through the top, batting and backing.

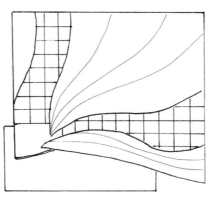

5: Position the lower border under the quilt. It will be offset 1¼" on the side and 2½" on the bottom. Keep it parallel to the top of the quilt. Pin in place.

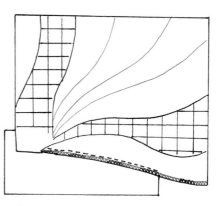

6: Again, topstitch along the inside of the serged stitches to attach the lower border to the quilt.

QUILT AND FINISH

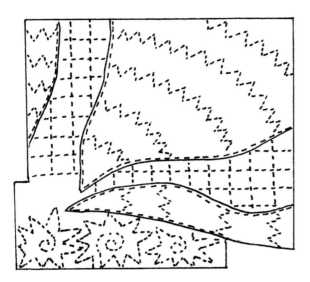

1: Quilt along the outside serged edge of the 3 background sections. Quilt the pieced segments by stitching in the ditch along the stitching lines. Quilt the purple background with radiating zigzag lines. Quilt spiraling stars in the lower border.

2: Using 2 binding strips cut from the backing fabric, stitch a faced binding to the sides and top of the quilt. Refer to *Quilting Terms & Techniques–Faced Binding* (page 24) for further instructions.

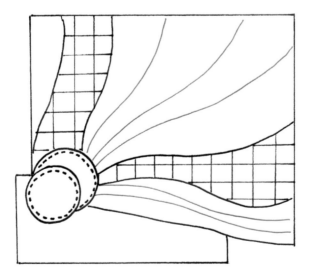

3: Lay the large circle in place on the previously-drawn chalk lines. Overlap with the smaller circle. If desired, place a slightly smaller circle of thin batting behind each circle to give additional puff and prevent shadowing-through of darker fabrics. Pin in place. Topstitch in place.

4: Position the butterflies. Hand-stitch in place.

5: Add a rod pocket and a label.

RESOURCES

AMERICAN AND EFIRD, INC.

Threads and yarns including Maxi-Lock® serger thread, Signature® Specialty threads, Signature® Quilting threads and Pixelles® threads.

P.O. Box 507
Mt. Holly, NC 28120
Phone: (800) 847-3235
Web: www.amefird.com

FAIRFIELD PROCESSING

Cotton and polyester fiber products for home and industry including earth-friendly BAMBOO batting.

P.O. Box 1130
Danbury, CT 06813-1130
Phone: (800) 980-8000
Web: www.poly-fil.com

FREE SPIRIT FABRICS

Producer of innovative quilt fabric designs including Katie Jump Rope, Urban Garden and Riviera.

Westminster Fibers Attn: Fabrics Division
3430 Toringdon Way, Suite 301
Charlotte, NC 28277
Phone: (866) 907-3305
Web: www.freespiritfabric.com

HOBBS BONDED FIBERS

Battings, pillow inserts and fiberfill including Heirloom® Premium cotton batting, Heirloom® 100% wool batting and Tuscany Collection cotton and wool batting.

P.O. Box 2521
Waco, TX 76702-2521
Phone: (800) 433-3357
Web: www.hobbsbondedfibers.com

PRESENCIA® HILATURAS USA

Threads for sewing, quilting, embroidery and crochet including Finca Perle Cotton and Presencia 50/3 and 40/3 cotton sewing thread.

P.O. Box 2409
Evergreen, CO 80437-2409
Phone: (888) 222-4523
Web: www.threads.com

PRYM CONSUMER USA

Sewing, quilting, cutting and craft-related tools and notions including Omnigrid® cutting tools, and Dritz quilting and sewing notions.

P.O. Box 5028
Spartanburg, SC 29304
Phone: (800) 845-4948
Web: www.dritz.com

ROBERT KAUFMAN CO., INC.

Fabric supplier and converter of quilting fabrics and textiles for manufacturers including greenSTYLE ecofriendly bamboo and bamboo/cotton prints.

129 W. 132nd St.
Los Angeles, CA 90061
Phone: (800) 877-2066
Web: www.robertkaufman.com

SUPERIOR THREADS

Quality threads for longarm and home machines including King Tut 40/3 cotton, Halo metallized textured polyester, So Fine! 50/3 polyester, and The Bottom Line 60 wt polyester.

P.O. Box 1672
St. George, Utah 84771
Phone: (800) 499-1777
Web: www.superiorthreads.com

THE WARM CO.

Batting and fusible products, including Warm & Safe Eco-Friendly Naturally Fire Retardant Batting and Lite Steam-A-Seam fusible web.

954 E. Union St.
Seattle, WA 98122
Phone: (800) 234-9276
Web: www.warmcompany.com

RECOMMENDED READING

Serge with Confidence BY NANCY ZIEMAN
Serging tips and techniques by sewing expert Nancy Zieman

Krause Publications
700 East State Street
Iola, WI, 54900-0001
Phone: (866) 457-2873
Web: www.krausebooks.com

INDEX

CAN'T STOP QUILTING? NEITHER CAN WE!

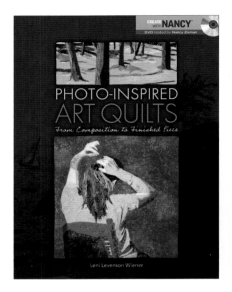

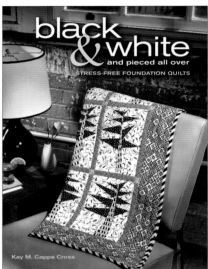

Photo-Inspired Art Quilts
From Composition to Finished Piece

Leni Levenson Wiener with Nancy Zieman

Grab your photos out of their frames and translate them in fabric. Leni Levenson teaches you how to choose photos for your quilt, turn them into fabric collage and embellish them with thread painting, raw-edge machine appliqué and other exciting techniques. As you work, you'll encounter tips from expert quilter Nancy Zieman. Nancy and Leni also bring you a DVD packed with a variety of construction approaches in action.

ISBN-10: 0-89689-804-0
ISBN-13: 978-0-89689-804-2
paperback, 128 pages, #Z2873

Black & White and Pieced All Over
Stress-Free Foundation Quilts

Kay M. Capps Cross

Black and white is bold and beautiful in this guide to stress-free foundation quilts. You'll achieve precision and perfection (without even trying!) as you work on 12 quilts in various sizes and with skill levels ranging from easiest to not hard. With just a splash of color, the black and white fabrics you'll work with allow you to focus on learning cross-cut techniques. The book's bonus CD includes all the project templates you'll need to begin foundation-piecing.

ISBN-10: 0-89689-942-X
ISBn-13: 978-0-89689-942-1
paperback, 128 pages, #Z3659

Log Cabin Quilts with Attitude
A New Twist on an Old Favorite

Sharon V. Rotz

Kiss your seam ripper goodbye! Enjoy quilting like never before as you disregard perfect seam allowances, forget about matching up corners and combine fabrics without fretting! Whether you want to use up your stash or splurge on brand-new fabrics, you'll revel in your newfound quilting freedom with *Log Cabin Quilts with Attitude*. Choose from more than 15 fun and fabulous projects, including bed quilts, banners, dining accessories, pillows, wall hangings and totes. You'll learn the basics of Freedom Blocks and then turn the traditional log cabin pattern on its ear.

ISBN-10: 0-89689-308-1
ISBN-13: 978-0-89689-308-5
paperback, 128 pages, #LCQA

Discover imagination, innovation and inspiration at www.mycraftivity.com. Connect. Create. Explore.